FAMILY TIME

TRAINING

Bible
Activities
and Object
Lessons
for Families
with
Children
of All Ages

Playing for Keeps

KIRK WEAVER

To Jim Weidmann, who introduced me to the priceless joy and peace that comes from providing intentional spiritual training in the home. To my family—Kelly, Madison, and McKinley—who have embraced Family Time as a core value in our life together. And, to our unborn grandchildren and great-grandchildren, may you learn, live, and teach Jesus as our personal Savior and eternal hope.

To Dave and Janet Pasque, who have provided encouragement, friendship, counsel, and support. Every step of the way—through challenges and successes—God has communicated his love and provision through Dave and Janet. Knowing Dave and Janet is one of the greatest blessings of my life.

—*Kirk Weaver*

Table of Contents

Just Imagine..6

Foreword..7

Introduction..8

The ABC's of Effective Family Times.........................10

Family Time Format...14

Family Activities

Lesson 1: SCRIPTURE CAKE...17
Teaching Goal: The Bible, God's Word, is food for our spirit.
Scripture: Matthew 4:4, John 4:34

Lesson 2: MODESTY..20
Teaching Goal: Modesty is dress that is pleasing to God.
Scripture: Genesis 2:21 to 3:11

Lesson 3: LUKEWARM SPIT..22
Teaching Goal: God wants our faith to be hot, not lukewarm.
Scripture: Revelation 3:15-16

Lesson 4: DEM BONES...25
Teaching Goal: Better times are coming for those who believe in God.
Scripture: Ezekiel 37:1-14

Lesson 5: RELATIONSHIP WITH GOD................................29
Teaching Goal: God wants a personal relationship with each of us.
Scripture: Genesis 3, Romans 3:23, John 3:16-17

Lesson 6: OBEDIENCE...32
Teaching Goal: We need to be obedient to God and to our parents.
Scripture: Ephesians 6:1, Romans 6:17, Genesis 18:19

Lesson 7: REPENTANCE..35
Teaching Goal: Repentance involves both an apology and changing our behavior.
Scripture: Acts 26:20, Acts 9, Jonah 2, 2 Kings 22-23

Lesson 8: THE HALL OF FAITH...39
Teaching Goal: Believing in God requires faith, and this is pleasing to God.
Scripture: Hebrews 11:6, Hebrews 11:1, Hebrews 11

Lesson 9: FIRM IN THE FAITH 43
Teaching Goal: Our surroundings can strengthen or weaken our faith.
Scripture: 1 Corinthians 15:33, 1 Corinthians 15:58,
Hebrews 10:25, Ephesians 6:10

Lesson 10: THE DOMINO EFFECT OF CHOICES 47
Teaching Goal: One person's choices may affect many other people
in good and bad ways.
Scripture: Genesis 15:1-5, Genesis 16:1-15, Genesis 17:18, 20,
Genesis 21:1-21, Genesis 25:8-9, 12-17

Lesson 11: DELAYED GRATIFICATION 54
Teaching Goal: Temporary discomfort can lead to greater rewards.
Scripture: Matthew 6:19-21, Matthew 5:11-12

Lesson 12: CHOCOLATE MILK 57
Teaching Goal: We need to let the Holy Spirit be our helper so
that Jesus can be part of everything in our lives.
Scripture: John 14:26, John 15:26, John 16:13

Lesson 13: BLINDED BY SIN 60
Teaching Goal: Sin can blind us and lead to more sin in our lives.
Scripture: 2 Corinthians 4:3-4, John 12:40, 1 John 2:10-11

Lesson 14: SPIRITUAL COFFEE 63
Teaching Goal: Christians are the fragrance of Christ in this world.
Scripture: 2 Corinthians 2:15-16

Lesson 15: BENT AND TORN 66
Teaching Goal: God is still with us and loves us when bad things happen.
Scripture: 2 Corinthians 11:16-33, 2 Corinthians 12:10,
2 Corinthians 4:8-9, Romans 8:28

Lesson 16: GOT YOU COVERED 70
Teaching Goal: Jesus' sacrifice on the cross covers our sin.
Scripture: Genesis 1:26, 2 Corinthians 5:17

Lesson 17: PLUMB LINE 74
Teaching Goal: As we build our lives, Christ is our foundation and
scripture is our "plumb line."
Scripture: Amos 7:7-8, Isaiah 28:16-17, 2 Timothy 3:16

Lesson 18: THE COMPANY WE KEEP 78
Teaching Goal: Be careful whom you hang around because bad
influences affect you.
Scripture: 1 Corinthians 15:33, Matthew 16:6, 2 Corinthians 6:14, 17

Lesson 19: ROCKS CRY OUT..82
Teaching Goal: All creation praises God.
Scripture: Luke 19:40, Hebrews 13:15

Lesson 20: PRAYING CONTINUALLY..85
Teaching Goal: We can talk to God anytime.
Scripture: 1 Samuel 1, 1 Samuel 1:12-13, 1 Thessalonians 5:17,
Ephesians 6:18

Lesson 21: AMBASSADOR..88
Teaching Goal: As a Christian, you represent Christ to non-Christians.
Scripture: Ephesians 6:19-20, 2 Corinthians 5:20, John 3:16

Topical Index of All Books 93
Contact Us 95

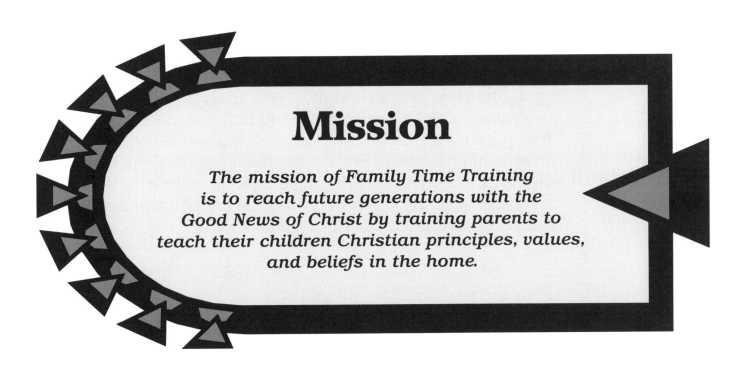

Mission

*The mission of Family Time Training
is to reach future generations with the
Good News of Christ by training parents to
teach their children Christian principles, values,
and beliefs in the home.*

Vision Statement

Imagine a child who responds to the needs of others and is eager to give and share.

Imagine a child who has learned to say "no" to busyness. A child who will take time to slow down and who understands the necessity of Sabbath rest.

Imagine a child who has been trained to seek truth.

Imagine a child who lives accountable to an unseen but always present God.

Imagine a child whose best friend is Jesus.

Imagine a child who is more eager to learn about the teachings of Jesus than to watch television or play sports.

Imagine a child with an eternal perspective, a child who invests more time giving and serving than accumulating and being entertained.

Imagine hundreds and thousands, a whole generation, of children growing up to live and teach the example of Christ.

In Deuteronomy 6:7 God presents his plan for passing on a godly heritage to our children. At Family Time Training our vision is to see future generations living for Christ. First, parents are to be the primary spiritual teachers in the lives of children. Second, spiritual training is to take place 24 hours a day, seven days a week. Family Time Training is just a tool, but it is a tool God can use in your family to accomplish his vision.

Foreword

"I believe most parents who are Christian want to teach their children the faith, they just don't know how. The church is important support but primary spiritual teaching must happen in the home, otherwise, it's not going to happen."

—R.C. Sproul, theologian

Family Time is the "how to" tool parents can use to teach their children the faith at home. The organization Family Time Training equips parents with fun and exciting activities designed to teach children Christian principles, values, and beliefs.

Family Time Training was formed in response to a spiritual crisis that threatens to undermine the foundation of today's families. For generations, Christian parents have abdicated to the church their God-given role as the primary spiritual leaders for their children. The church is expected to build within the lives of children a strong spiritual foundation in just one or two hours per week. God designed spiritual training to take place 24 hours a day, seven days a week, with the parents providing primary leadership and the church providing important support. For the sake of our children we must return proactive spiritual training to the home.

Family Time Training works with churches, schools, and spiritually-based groups to teach parents how to provide home-based spiritual training. Training is provided through sermons, classes, and weekend seminars. Families receive direct support through a website (www.famtime.com), activity books, and quarterly mailings.

—Kirk Weaver

Introduction

Not long ago, my wife Kelly and I were talking with Madison on her bed in her room. She was upset with the kids at school. Some were picking on an unpopular student, playing a cruel game Madi chose not to play, and it left her separated from her girlfriends. With tears flowing down her face, Madi said, "I'm trying to be like the beans in Dad's story."

Madi was referring to a Family Time lesson. The activity is built around three pots of boiling water, with the water representing adversity. We drop a carrot into the first pot, an egg into the second, and coffee beans into the third. What choices will we make in response to the adversity we face in our lives? Do we get soft like the carrot the way Peter did when he denied Christ? Does the adversity make us hard like the egg and Pharaoh's heart? Or like the coffee beans, which can represent the example of Paul, do we influence and change the environment around us? Madi was applying a lesson that we'd taught more than four months earlier.

As a parent, you've had moments like this. You know what they're worth.

Family Time activities are simple, fun object lessons intended to teach children about life in God's world. This is a book of ideas for structured teaching times that will carry forward and open doors for informal learning moments. At first it may feel a little clumsy to create the structured time, to boil carrots and eggs and coffee beans. But the moments when your child actively chooses the godly path will fuel your love and your relationship like nothing else in the world.

"Here's the game," I told the four children, my son, daughter, and two neighborhood friends. They were standing at the bottom of the stairs, wide-eyed and eager for the Family Time activity. Standing at the top of the stairs, I said, "I represent Jesus in heaven. More than anything I want you up here with me, but, you can't use the stairs and you can't use the handrails."

They knew there was a trick, something to learn. But what? How would they get from the bottom of the stairs to the top without touching the stairs or the railing? My daughter ran to get a laundry basket, turned it upside down, stood on top and reached up only to find she was still more than fifteen steps from the top.

It was my son, Mac, the youngest of the four, who figured out the solution. "I got it! Dad, please come down and get me," his face beaming, because he had solved the riddle. I descended the stairs.

"Will you carry me to the top?" he asked. "Of course!" I responded. After carrying all four children piggyback style to the second floor, I said, "That's how you get to heaven. You can't do it on your own. Only through Jesus can you get there." A powerful lesson presented in the language of children that they still remember to this day.

Deuteronomy 6:5-9 says:
> *"Love the LORD your God with all your heart and with all your soul and with all your strength. These commandments that I give you today are to be upon your hearts. Impress them on your children."*

How?
> *"Talk about them when you sit at home and when you walk along the road, when you lie down and when you get up. Tie them as symbols on your hands and bind them on your foreheads. Write them on the doorframes of your houses and on your gates."*

How will we shape our children? What mark will we leave upon them? Is it possible that we can launch them into the world stronger, purer, more trusting of God than we were? Is it possible that we can reshape our families and our family interactions around the joy of loving God with all that is within us?

I believe it is possible. That's what this book is for.

The 's of Effective Family Times

A **Attention Span:** The rule of thumb for attention span is one minute for each year of age. A three-year-old may have a three-minute attention span. Break up your Family Time into three-minute increments. With variety, you gain additional attention span. For example:

3 minutes	Sing or play your Family Time theme song
2 minutes	Pray
3 minutes	Tell the story
3 minutes	Demonstrate the object lesson
3 minutes	Let the child repeat the object lesson
3 minutes	Retell the story
2 minutes	Practice memorization
2 minutes	Close in prayer

21 minutes	Total Family Time

B **Be Prepared to Say "I Don't Know":** Your children WILL ask you a question that you cannot answer. Promise to find the answer and get back to them within 24 hours. You can call a pastor or search the Internet for more information.

C **Call it Family Time:** When your children grow up you want them to have fond, lasting memories of Family Time. When referring to your times of formal spiritual training, say "Family Time" often. In the same way your children will remember going to school and church or playing sports and music, they will remember times of spiritual training called "Family Time."

D **Drama Queens and Kings:** Kids love to put on plays. Pick a Bible Story, assign the roles from Director to Diva—everyone gets in on the act. Don't forget to assign a videographer so you can watch it later.

E ▶ **Encourage Guessing:** Answering a question involves risk. Your child's answer may be right or wrong. Praise him when he guesses at an answer. If he gives the wrong answer say, "Great guess! The answer is..." and give him the correct information. This will keep him participating. If you say, "No, that's wrong," children may eventually stop talking.

F ▶ **Fixed or Flexible:** It's great and admirable to have Family Time the same night every week. However, it may not be practical for your family. Be willing to move the night if needed. The important thing is to have at least one Family Time each week.

G ▶ **Give it to God:** God commands parents and grandparents to be spiritual teachers with their children (Deuteronomy 6:7; Deuteronomy 4:9, Psalm 78:5). Trust that God will equip you to fulfill his plan. As you prepare, and before you begin your Family Time each week, pray and ask the Holy Spirit to lead you and clearly communicate the message to your children.

H ▶ **Hold the Distractions:** When sitting at the table, remove the centerpiece, pencils, paper...anything that can distract a child. A random paper clip left on a table can lead to a possession battle that will ruin the atmosphere for Family Time. Also, when using materials like balloons, string, etc., don't bring them out until you're ready to use them.

I ▶ **Involve Kids in the Preparations:** Whenever possible, especially as kids get a little older, involve kids in the lesson preparations. Preparation can be as much fun as doing the activity and certainly increases ownership. Kids will enjoy making an obstacle course, building a tent with sheets, or mixing a big batch of cornstarch.

J ▶ **Just Do It!:** Don't wait another day to get started!

K ▶ **Kitchen Table:** Start your Family Time at the kitchen table even if you are only going to be there for a few minutes. Chairs provide natural boundaries that will help children focus as you explain what will happen during the Family Time.

L **Listen to the Holy Spirit:** Be prepared to modify or change the discussion if the Spirit moves the conversation in a different direction.

M **Make a Picture:** Coloring a picture to reinforce a Bible Story can be an excellent teaching technique. While the family is coloring, great conversation about the lesson can take place.

N **Not a Spectator Sport:** Participate with your children in the game or activity. By participating, you show your kids that you value Family Time.

O **Oh Boy!** If you're feeling frustrated or if family members have a negative attitude—reschedule. Keep it positive.

P **Play it Again, Sam:** For younger children, put the lesson into a one sentence phrase like: "Noah had faith in God." Or, "Be content with what God sent." The same night at bedtime, remind children of the main point. The following morning ask them what they remember from Family Time the night before.

Q **Quitting isn't an Option:** Commit to once a week and do your best not to take a week off. Continue to do Family Time during the summer months. If you stop, your kids will sense a lack of commitment to Family Time on your part.

R **Repetition isn't the Same as Redundant:** Younger children learn best through repetition. In the same way they will watch a video over and over, they may want to repeat fun Family Time activities. Be prepared to repeat the activity, asking the children to explain what the different elements represent. Consider repeating with neighborhood children; your children will learn even more when they teach others.

S **Simple Structure:** Younger children benefit from a structured time together. Consider following the Family Time Format each week.

T **To Be or Not to Be Silly:** Model for your children that it's okay to be dramatic, silly, and have fun. Kids love it when their parents are playful.

U **Unique Locations:** Have a church service in a crawl space to represent the early church under persecution. Hold your Family Time outside at a neighborhood park. Repeat fun activities when visiting relatives on vacation. Tell the story of Zacchaeus while sitting in a tree house. Changing the setting of your Family Time can be fun.

V **Variety:** Using a video clip can be an excellent way to teach a lesson. However, using video clips three weeks in a row becomes predictable and is less effective. Mix up the format and tools you use in your weekly Family Time (coloring, video clips, a snack tied to the lesson, etc.).

W **Watch Out for Unrealistic Expectations:** Family Time is seldom a disappointment to children. However, parents may sometimes feel like the lesson did not go as well as they had hoped. Often this disappointment is directly related to the parent's expectations. Keep in mind that kids learn valuable things over time. You don't have to get something fantastic out of each Family Time. Be prepared to learn right along with your kids.

X **Xpect a Future:** One day your children will grow up and start families of their own. As your children raise your grandchildren they will be equipped with positive memories and effective tools to pass along the faith of their fathers.

Y **Y? Y? Y?** Questions are cool. Frederick Beuchner says, "If you want big answers then ask small questions." "What did you learn at Sunday School?" is a big question. "Who did you sit next to at Sunday School?" is a smaller question that can lead to more discussion.

Z **Zees ees Fun!** Remember the most important things you can do: take your time, engage your child, and have fun together. A silly accent never hurts either!

Family Time Format

The "Family Time Format" is a simple structure that families can use when leading a Family Time activity. You may want to tweak and modify the structure to meet the needs of your family.

Younger children benefit from using the same format from week to week. They may want to repeat the activity again and again. Remember, repetition is how young children learn. Be sure to call your time together "Family Time." When your kids are grown, you want them to look back and be able to identify times of formal spiritual training in the same way they can identify school, sports, and church.

Families of older children may want to make the lesson less formal. For example, you may not have a "Family Time Theme Song." Instead, you can invite your teens to share a favorite song. Ask them why they like the song. Is it the beat, the singer, the words?

Meet Weekly:
The goal is to lead a weekly Family Time in your home. Try to designate and reserve the same time each week, recognizing that on occasion you will need the flexibility to schedule around conflicts.

No Fuss Dinner:
Plan a simple dinner so that everyone in the family can participate. You don't want one parent spending a lot of time fixing the meal and another parent spending a lot of time cleaning up. Minimize dinner preparation and clean-up by using paper plates and paper cups. Just by looking at how the table is set, children will know it's Family Time night. You may want to use leftovers or order in dinner. Keep it simple.

Discuss the Previous Family Time:
During dinner talk about what the family did last week during Family Time. Challenge the children to try and remember the activity and message. Talk about the

highlights and use this time to reinforce the message and its potential application during the past week.

You'll be surprised to learn that children will remember back two weeks, three weeks, maybe more.

Family Time Theme Song:

Pick your own family "theme song." Since this is for your spiritual training time, consider songs that talk about faith, family, relationships, and love.

Play this song after dinner and just before the evening lesson and activity. Younger children like to create a dance or hand motions to go with the song. This song signals that Family Time is here while building excitement and anticipation.

SONG IDEAS:
"The Family Prayer Song (As For Me and My House)" by Maranatha
"Creed" by Rich Mullins

Prayer:

Open the Family Time with prayer. Children and parents can take turns. Teach the children to pray about a wide variety of topics, joys, and concerns.

Message:

Decide in advance and practice the activity you will use. Communicate clearly the main principle or value being taught through the lesson.

Object Lesson:

Each Family Time has an object lesson or activity that reinforces and helps children remember the main message.

Memorize:

Repeat the short, rhyming phrase included with the lesson. The rhyme is designed to help children remember the lesson.

Prayer:

Close the time together with a prayer. Tie the prayer to the lesson. Try different methods of prayer such as holding hands and praying, pray from oldest to youngest, or say "popcorn" prayers (one- or two-word prayers about a specific topic).

Plan Ahead for Next Week:

Many lessons require that you gather specific objects or purchase items from the store. Look ahead to next week's Family Time activity to make sure you have all the necessary ingredients.

Lesson 1:
SCRIPTURE CAKE

 TEACHING GOAL: The Bible, God's Word, is food for our spirit.

1. Play theme song
2. Pray
3. Lesson and discussion
4. Memorize: **Food our belly fills; the Bible our spirit builds.**
5. Close in prayer

SCRIPTURE: Matthew 4:4 "Man does not live on bread alone, but on every word that comes from the mouth of God."

John 4:34 "'My food,' said Jesus, 'is to do the will of him who sent me and to finish his work.'"

MATERIALS: Flour, butter, sugar, honey, milk, eggs, almonds, raisins, baking powder, spices, salt
Mixing bowls
Measuring cups and spoons
Cake pan
Beater
Oven

Words that are written in **bold** are when you, the parent, are speaking. Feel free to use your own words.

Big Idea

Read the scripture verses and talk about different "foods." **There is the food that we eat that gives us energy. Gas is food for a car. Exercise is food for our muscles. God gave us the Bible, his Word, to feed our spirits.**

 **Activity**

Baking a cake. **We are going to make a cake using foods that are mentioned in God's Word.**

Older children can be given the list of food items and use a concordance to look up scriptures that mention the food item. Or they can be given the scriptures and take turns finding them in the Bible.

Parents can read each verse to younger children and have the child pick out the food. Then the child can help measure the food into the mixing bowls and assist with the baking.

Spice Cake

RECIPE: Cream butter and sugar together. Add honey and eggs. In another bowl, mix flour, baking powder, spices, and salt. Add to butter mixture and mix well. Add milk gradually. Beat well. Fold in almonds and raisins if desired. Bake in greased and floured cake pan at 350 degrees for one hour.

3 c	Fine Flour	1 Kings 4:22	NIV
1/2 c	Butter	Proverbs 30:33	NIV
1 c	Sugar	Jeremiah 6:20	KJV
1 c	Honey	Judges 14:8	NIV
1/2 c	Milk	1 Peter 2:2	NIV
6	Eggs	Luke 11:12	NIV
2 c	Almonds (chopped)	Numbers 17:8	NIV
2 c	Raisins	2 Samuel 16:1	NIV
2 T	Baking powder (leaven)	1 Corinthians 5:6	KJV
1/2 t	Salt	Leviticus 2:13	NIV

Spices (cinnamon, nutmeg, cloves)

Or, you may choose to give older children the recipe in "code."

Spice Cake

Cream $1/2$ c of Proverbs 30:33 and mix with 1 c of Jeremiah 6:20 (KJV) together. Add 6 of Luke 11:12 and 1 c of Judges 14:8. In another bowl, mix 3 c of 1 Kings 4:22, 2 T of 1 Corinthians 5:6 (KJV), and $1/2$ t of Leviticus 2:13. Add spices. Add the two mixtures and mix well. Add $1/2$ c of 1 Peter 2:2 gradually. Beat well. Fold in 2 c of chopped Numbers 17:8 and 2 c of 2 Samuel 16:1 if desired. Bake in greased and floured cake pan at 350 degrees for one hour.

Mix the cake before dinner. Put the cake in the oven and eat dinner. Watch a Christian video while the cake is cooling. Eat the cake for dessert.

◖C▸ Application

Cake sure is good, isn't it? It satisfies us and we feel good after we eat it. The same thing is true in our spiritual lives. Reading the Bible gives us nourishment for our spirits. Many people make a practice of reading the Bible every day. When they do they get the spiritual food they need to face life's challenges.

Take time and thank God for his Word.

Lesson 2:
MODESTY

TEACHING GOAL: Modesty is dress that is pleasing to God.

1. Play theme song
2. Pray
3. Review last lesson
4. Lesson and discussion
5. Memorize: **When I begin my day and start to dress; I think of God and what he'd bless.**
   or
   In all I do I'll show I care; this includes the clothes I wear.
6. Close in prayer

SCRIPTURE: Genesis 2:21 to 3:11 The story of God creating Eve to be with Adam. They were both naked and not ashamed. The serpent tempts them to eat the forbidden fruit. Adam and Eve realize they are naked and cover themselves.

MATERIALS: Popular magazines like:
People, TV Guide, Fashion
Paper
Something to write with
Green and red colored markers

Words that are written in **bold** are when you, the parent, are speaking. Feel free to use your own words.

A▶ Big Idea

Tell the story of Adam and Eve at an age-appropriate level for your children. Emphasize the parts about being naked and covering themselves.

Discussions about modesty are important because they give you opportunity to talk about values and convictions. Furthermore, children often want to emulate the latest clothing styles, many of which are immodest, thus giving you opportunity to talk about the differences between your values and those of the world.

 **Activity**

Flip through the pages of one or two magazines looking for pictures of people who are dressed modestly and immodestly.

Make a list of reasons why some clothes are modest and why others are immodest. Some outfits are chosen because the wearer wants to draw attention to himself or herself—their clothes are saying "look at me." Make a green dot with a marker on clothes that are modest or appropriate. Make a red dot with a marker on clothes that are immodest or saying "look at me."

OPTIONAL FOR OLDER CHILDREN
Go to the mall for a "window shopping" trip and look at all the latest fashions. Discuss what the wearer is silently communicating by wearing certain outfits. Some stores cater more to a certain style or message. What message do we want to give with the clothes we wear?

 **Application**

- **What type of modest and immodest clothing do you see at school?**
- **Why would wearing a swimsuit at the beach be okay but might be immodest at church or work?**
- **Did you know there are other countries where women cover their faces except for their eyes and completely cover their legs? It would be immodest for them to have bare legs in public.**

Christian families may disagree on what is modest and immodest. How are you going to handle dressing in a way that Mom and Dad feel is appropriate when friends and others choose to dress differently?

Lesson 3:
LUKEWARM SPIT

TEACHING GOAL: God wants our faith to be hot, not lukewarm.

1. Play theme song
2. Pray
3. Review last lesson
4. Lesson and discussion
5. Memorize: **To God be true; he won't spit you.**
6. Close in prayer

SCRIPTURE: Revelation 3:15-16 "I know your deeds, that you are neither cold nor hot. I wish you were either one or the other! So, because you are lukewarm —neither hot nor cold—I am about to spit you out of my mouth."

MATERIALS: Small paper cups
Salt, sugar, water

IN ADVANCE: For each family member, fill three small paper cups 2/3 full with water (if you have four family members then you will need 12 cups). Leave one cup with plain water, in the second cup add sugar, and in the third cup add salt. Keep the cups to the side until you need them. **YOU WILL WANT TO DO THIS ACTIVITY OUTSIDE OR NEAR A SINK.**

Words that are written in **bold** are when you, the parent, are speaking. Feel free to use your own words.

 **Big Idea**

In the book of Revelation, God writes a special letter to a church in the town of Laodicea. In the letter, God compares the people in the church to different temperatures of water—cold, hot, and lukewarm. A "cold" person is someone who doesn't follow God. A "hot" person is

someone who tries hard to follow God. The "lukewarm" person is someone who says they follow God (hot) but their actions are bad (cold).

God tells the people in Laodicea that they are lukewarm and he wants to spit them out of his mouth! God is not happy with the people in this church. In fact, God says he wishes they were hot or cold, instead of lukewarm.

I can understand why God would want them to be hot—trying hard to follow God, but why would he want them cold—not following God, instead of lukewarm? Listen to answers.

There is a great danger in being lukewarm. The lukewarm person will deceive you.

Consider hot, cold, and lukewarm friends. I like it when you are with kids who make good choices (that's like being hot). I don't like you to be around kids who make bad choices (that's like being cold). But what about the kid who acts good on the outside but pressures you to do things you shouldn't (that's like lukewarm)? If you see someone who is making bad choices then you know to stay away. However, you may be deceived and get into serious trouble when someone acts nice at first and then pressures you into doing things you know you shouldn't do.

BE CAUTIOUS OF PEOPLE WHO SAY ONE THING AND THEN ACT ANOTHER WAY!

B▶ Activity

We are going to play a game which involves spitting. When you spit, be sure to use the sink (or spit to a designated place outside). We will take turns playing this game. Each family member will have three cups. One cup is filled with plain water and that represents being "cold." Another cup has sugar water and that represents being "hot." The third cup has salt water and that represents being "lukewarm." If you pick the cup with hot or cold water then you drink the liquid and you get to keep the cup, that counts as one point. If you pick the cup with salt water then spit it out because it will taste nasty. You get no point if you pick the salt water cup. The one with the most cups (points) at the end is the winner.

Mix up each person's three cups before they make their pick. **CAUTION:** Encourage younger kids to take a sip. They will not like a mouth full of salt water!

The two cups that are not used in each turn can be reused for a second and third turn. After everyone has had a turn, set all the leftover cups off to the side. Now select three at random and give each person a second turn. You may have no salt water cups in this turn or you may have two or three! As each person's turn is over return the leftover cups to the side and repeat until all the cups have been used.

Application

We want to be "hot" Christians. We want people to know we are Christians by what we say and by what we do. We do not want to be "lukewarm" people who say good things but then do bad things. And we want to be cautious of others who are lukewarm.

Lesson 4:
DEM BONES

TEACHING GOAL: Better times are coming for those who believe in God.

1. Play theme song
2. Pray
3. Review last lesson
4. Lesson and discussion
5. Memorize: **Dem bones gonna rise again; better times lie around the bend.**
6. Close in prayer

SCRIPTURE: Ezekiel 37:1-14 Ezekiel's vision in the Valley of Dry Bones.

MATERIALS: Packing peanuts (must be cornstarch based)—Craft stores sell them as "Magic Noodles"
Sponge—moist

Words that are written in **bold** are when you, the parent, are speaking. Feel free to use your own words.

 **Big Idea**

If you know the tune to the old spiritual, teach the family and sing "Dem Bones." **In the 1800's it was legal for families in America to own slaves. Often the slaves were treated terribly—they were beaten, parents were separated from their children—life was very hard. Many slaves were Christians who had a strong faith in Jesus. Their faith kept them going during tough times. Slaves would sing songs of hope. Dem Bones is a slave song that is still popular today.** Sing and add hand motions by touching the different body parts named in the song.

DEM BONES

Written By: Unknown

Ezekiel cried, "Dem dry bones!"
Ezekiel cried, "Dem dry bones!"
Ezekiel cried, "Dem dry bones!"
"Oh, hear the word of the Lord."
The foot bone connected to the leg bone,
The leg bone connected to the knee bone,
The knee bone connected to the thigh bone,
The thigh bone connected to the back bone,
The back bone connected to the neck bone,
The neck bone connected to the head bone,
Oh, hear the word of the Lord!
Dem bones, dem bones, gonna walk aroun'
Dem bones, dem bones, gonna walk aroun'
Dem bones, dem bones, gonna walk aroun'
Oh, hear the word of the Lord!
The head bone connected to the neck bone,
The neck bone connected to the back bone,
The back bone connected to the thigh bone,
The thigh bone connected to the knee bone,
The knee bone connected to the leg bone,
The leg bone connected to the foot bone,
Oh, hear the word of the Lord!

This song is based on a Bible story. The story is found in the book of Ezekiel and it's called "The Valley of the Dry Bones."

 **Activity**

In your own words, tell the story of Ezekiel in the Valley of the Dry Bones. **In a vision God took Ezekiel to the middle of a valley filled with dry bones. God asked Ezekiel, "Can these dry bones live?" Ezekiel gave a smart answer. He said, "Only you know, God." God told Ezekiel, "Tell these bones that they will come to life. I will put tendons and muscles on the bones and cover the muscles with skin.**

I will breath life into them and they will live and know that I am God!" Ezekiel said to the bones what God had said. The bones came together; they were still dead until God breathed life into them. The bones stood up and formed a large army.

Ezekiel lived at a time when God's children, the Israelites, had been captured and were living as prisoners and slaves in a foreign country, Babylon. Family members and friends had been killed so only a few Israelites remained.

God told Ezekiel that the bones represented the remaining Israelites. They felt dead. They felt like there was no hope. They were sad about family members and friends who had died. They were living as prisoners in a foreign land. Just like God breathed life into the dry bones, God promised the Israelites that he was going to save them from Babylon. They were going to go back home to their own land. Good times were ahead.

Spread the packing peanuts over the table. Place the damp sponge so that everyone can reach it. **This is the valley filled with dry bones. The moisture in the sponge represents the breath of God. Tap the end**

of a peanut on the sponge (damp, not wet) **and connect it to another peanut. Continue until you build a person.**

OPTIONAL: Practice singing the song while you build people out of the dry bones.

 Application

The lesson from this story for us today is that no matter how bad things seem, better times are coming for Christians who love God. Keep your hope in God who is able to deliver you from bad times. Family members can share their experiences with difficult times.

Looking back, can you see God helping you through the hard times? Maybe like the Israelites you are still in the middle of difficult times. (Even when sickness takes the life of someone we love, we have God's promise of life without pain waiting for us in heaven.)

Lesson 5:
RELATIONSHIP WITH GOD

TEACHING GOAL: God wants a personal relationship with each of us.

1. Play theme song
2. Pray
3. Review last lesson
4. Lesson and discussion
5. Memorize: **Keep Jesus in your heart; so you don't grow apart.**
6. Close in prayer

SCRIPTURE: Genesis 3 God's relationship with Adam and Eve.

Romans 3:23 "For all have sinned and fall short of the glory of God."

John 3:16-17 "For God so loved the world that he gave his one and only Son, that whoever believes in him shall not perish but have eternal life. For God did not send his Son into the world to condemn the world, but to save the world through him."

MATERIALS: 3 strips of newspaper—approximately 2″ x 3′
Tape and scissors

Words that are written in **bold** are when you, the parent, are speaking. Feel free to use your own words.

 Big Idea

In your own words, explain that God had a special relationship with Adam and Eve before they sinned. There were no secrets, no pain, no bad times before sin. When Adam and Eve disobeyed God and ate from the tree of life, sin entered the world. Now Adam and Eve were afraid of God, they felt guilt, shame, pain, and death. Every person since Adam and Eve has been a sinner (read Romans 3:23).

B Activity

Form a circle by taping the two ends of the first strip of newspaper together. Make sure *not to twist* the paper. **This circle of paper represents the relationship Adam and Eve had with God before they sinned. Their relationship was like a family in which people are close, love each other, know a lot about each other, and really trust each other. I'm going to cut this paper down the middle to show how sin separated Adam and Eve from God.** Poke the scissors in the middle of the paper circle and cut the strip long-ways down the middle, creating two separate circles. **See how sin separates God and man? These circles represent people who are separated from God.**

God loves us and wants us to be with him. God sent his son, Jesus, to give his life for us and take away our sin so we can be back together with God. There are people who know about Jesus, believe he is the Son of God, and have a relationship with him. There are also people who know about Jesus, they have knowledge of him, but they do not believe he is the Son of God.

Take another strip of paper and this time twist one end one full twist (360 degrees) so that the same side is facing up again. (Do not draw attention to making the twist. The child should be surprised at a different result when the paper is cut.) Tape the ends together into a circle. Begin to cut long-ways through the circle. You will end up with two circles but they will be linked together. **How are these circles different from the last two we cut? These circles are linked together, not separated. The linked circles represent people who have heard about Jesus but they don't know him personally. They are "connected" through knowledge but not through a relationship.**

When we recognize that we are sinners, believe that Jesus is the Son of God, and ask him to forgive us, then something very different happens! We begin a relationship with Jesus. His Spirit begins to work inside us. We learn more about Jesus and piece by piece we turn our lives over to him. We are no longer separated from Jesus and we have more than knowledge—now we have a relationship!

Take the third strip of paper and make a *half twist* (180 degrees) so that the top of one end is touching the back of the other end and tape into a circle. Cut through the center as before. This time one solid large circle will result. **What is different about the circle this time?** There is one circle, not two. **With Jesus in our lives we can again have a relationship with God just like he had with Adam and Eve before sin entered the world.**

Application

God wants to have a personal relationship with us. That means he wants us to relate to him every day. How does someone have a relationship with God? (Be prepared to help your child understand what salvation means personally.) **One of the ways we nurture that relationship with God is by praying and talking with God regularly. Let's pray now and thank God for loving us and inviting us to enjoy relationship with him.**

Lesson 6:
OBEDIENCE

TEACHING GOAL: We need to be obedient to God and to our parents.

1. Play theme song
2. Pray
3. Review last lesson
4. Lesson and discussion
5. Memorize: **When we obey right away; then there's time left for play.**
6. Close in prayer

SCRIPTURE: Ephesians 6:1 "Children, obey your parents in the Lord, for this is right."

Romans 6:17 "But thanks be to God that, though you used to be slaves to sin, you wholeheartedly obeyed the form of teaching to which you were entrusted."

Genesis 18:19 "For I have chosen him, so that he will direct his children and his household after him to keep the way of the LORD by doing what is right and just, so that the LORD will bring about for Abraham what he has promised him."

MATERIALS: Large jar
Birdseed
Golf balls or ping pong balls (approx. 12)
Small plastic bags and masking tape
Bowl or pitcher

IN ADVANCE: In order to determine how much birdseed is needed, place the 12 balls in the jar, and fill the remainder of the jar with birdseed. Now take the balls and birdseed out of the jar and divide the birdseed into plastic bags.

Words that are written in **bold** are when you, the parent, are speaking. Feel free to use your own words.

 **Big Idea**

Doesn't it seem like there's so many things we can do in a day and we just run out of time sometimes? And then there are times when parents have ideas of things we should do too. How can we fit all these things into our lives?

Part of the solution is to plan our time and our lives so that we can get the most important things done. In today's activity we'll get an idea of how we can do just that.

 **Activity**

The jar represents the amount of time everyone has each week. We all have the same amount of time. The birdseed represents things we do that we enjoy, but that take up lots of time. Ask your children to name their favorite activities. Bike riding, playing with friends, coloring, etc. Write each activity on a piece of tape and label each bag of birdseed.

Empty the bags of birdseed into the jar as you talk to the children again about what each bag of birdseed represents and show them how much time these activities take each week.

There are other activities, chores, and responsibilities we need to do every day or every week.

TASK	WHY
Clean up room	Take care of what we have
	Avoid tripping and being hurt
Wash: bath, teeth, hair	Health: avoid sickness
	Won't smell bad
Clean up dishes after dinner	Help family
	Obey parents

TASK	WHY
Make bed	Help family
	Obey parents
Family Time	Parents teach children
	Learn about God
Sunday School	Learn about God
School	Learn
Homework	Learn

The balls represent the tasks we need to do for God and parents every day or every week. At times we may not want to do some of these activities, but we need to be obedient. Talk about the tasks and why it is important to do them. Explain that the balls represent the amount of time the tasks take. All the balls will not fit into the jar.

Take the balls back out and dump the birdseed into the bowl or pitcher. **But, if we obey God and our parents and do what they ask us to do first,** (place the balls in the empty jar) **then there will still be enough time to do our other activities** (pour in the birdseed). **It all fits.**

EXAMPLE: When a child fusses in the morning before school about getting dressed, eating breakfast, or combing hair, then it may take 40 minutes to do what can be done in 15 minutes. Because he did not obey right away, there wasn't time to play.

 **Application**

Knowing how to manage our time is very important and it's a sign of someone who is mature and growing up. Some people just complain and complain about how much time they don't have. Or they manage their time so poorly that others are disappointed with them because they can't get the most important things done. Remember that if you plan the most important things first, then all the other things can fit around them.

Lesson 7:
REPENTANCE

TEACHING GOAL: Repentance involves both an apology and changing our behavior.

1. Play theme song
2. Pray
3. Review last lesson
4. Lesson and discussion
5. Memorize: **Sorry + changed behavior = repentance**
6. Close in prayer

SCRIPTURE: Acts 26:20 "I preached that they should repent and turn to God and prove their repentance by their deeds."

Acts 9 Paul, who has denied Jesus as Lord, calls him Lord and stops persecuting Christians.

Jonah 2 Jonah calls out to God from inside the fish and changes his way by going to Nineveh to deliver God's message.

2 Kings 22-23 Josiah finds the Book of the Law, prays to the Lord for forgiveness, and destroys the idols throughout the land.

MATERIALS: String
Washer
Bolt or screw
Scissors

Words that are written in **bold** are when you, the parent, are speaking. Feel free to use your own words.

◢A Big Idea

What does the word repent mean? Listen to their answers. **To repent is to acknowledge doing something wrong plus changing what you are doing from wrong to right. Repentance requires both an apology and a change in behavior. Can you think of an example of repentance?** Paul, Jonah, Josiah, etc.

◢B Activity

Plan this situation in advance, before you start your Family Time. Role-play with two adults or an adult and one of the older children. Sitting close to each other, one adult gently kicks the other's leg with his foot. The kicker says, "Sorry, I didn't mean to kick you," but a few seconds later he kicks again followed by "Sorry." Repeat this kicking and apologizing situation four times.

The person being kicked asks the rest of the family: **Do you think he is really sorry for kicking me? Why or why not? He is saying the words but is he changing his actions? He is apologizing, but without changing his action he is not repenting.**

God tells us to repent. God is pleased when we say we are sorry and we change our ways and do what is right.

Take a piece of string. This string represents our relationship to God. Tie a washer on one end.

This washer represents God. Tie a bolt or screw on the other end. **This screw represents us.** The distance between the washer and screw should be approximately two feet. Measure the distance with the ruler. **The scissors represent sin.**

Holding the string in the air by the washer, use the scissors to cut the string. **When we sin it feels like we are farther away from God. We feel a gap in our relationship, guilt from doing something wrong.**

Lay the cut pieces of string end to end. **But as Christians we have Jesus who has already paid the price for our sins through his death on the cross. Because of Jesus there is no gap in our relationship with God.**

Tie a knot to put the cut ends back together. **When we repent, say we are sorry, and change our actions, we are doing what God asks us to do. Because we are doing what God asks, we actually end up feeling closer to God. The knot represents repentance and the restored relationship with God.**

Repeat the cutting of the string and tying the ends together. After doing it several times measure the string with the ruler. The distance between the washer and the bolt or screw is shorter. **Just like the string, our relationship with God is closer when we do what he asks us to do about sin— repent.**

 **Application**

Now, let's go back to our first question again. What is repentance? It involves both saying you're sorry and making a change in your behavior. **God wants us to work on areas of our lives and grow in our maturity. Sometimes that change doesn't come easily. It takes time, and while we are growing we can sometimes get angry with ourselves or feel discouraged. It's especially valuable at those times**

to come to God and tell him that we're sorry. We can ask him for strength to do the right thing and then we can practice doing what's right.

That process of asking God to help us grow is very important because it moves us closer to God. Some people believe that they have to be perfect in order to talk to God, but that's not true. God wants us to come to him at any time to learn and to grow.

Lesson 8:
THE HALL OF FAITH

TEACHING GOAL: Believing in God requires faith, and this is pleasing to God.

1. Play theme song
2. Pray
3. Review last lesson
4. Lesson and discussion
5. Memorize: **Listed in the Hall of Faith is me; because I'm certain of God and heaven that I cannot see.**
6. Close in prayer

SCRIPTURE: Hebrews 11:6 "And without faith it is impossible to please God, because anyone who comes to him must believe that he exists and that he rewards those who earnestly seek him."

Hebrews 11:1 "Now faith is being sure of what we hope for and certain of what we do not see."

Hebrews 11 This chapter is the Hall of Faith in the Bible.

MATERIALS: Paper and markers
Sports cards (your own, borrow or buy)
Camera

Words that are written in **bold** are when you, the parent, are speaking. Feel free to use your own words.

 Big Idea

Start by saying, **"Name the best professional sports athlete you know."** Stick with the sport of the athlete named first. So, if the first child to answer says, "John Elway," then say, **"Okay, let's stick with football and everyone gets a chance to name a great football player."**

On a piece of paper where the children can see, make a list of the football players they name. Parents can feed name suggestions to younger children. After everyone has had an opportunity to add a name to the list, ask, **"Who is the best football player?"**

Circle the one they agree is the best. If there is a debate, then you may want to circle more than one player.

Repeat the listing of names for a few other sports such as baseball, basketball, tennis, etc. At the end, you should have several lists with at least one name circled in each list.

 **Activity**

Did you know there is a special honor for athletes who are considered to be one of the best players of their sport? After they stop playing and retire, the best athletes have their names included in the Hall of Fame. For older children you might ask where various Halls of Fame are located.

Baseball:	Cooperstown, New York
Football:	Canton, Ohio
Basketball:	Springfield, Massachusetts
Bowling:	St. Louis, Missouri
Rodeo:	Colorado Springs, Colorado
Cowboy:	Oklahoma City, Oklahoma
Gymnastics:	Oklahoma City, Oklahoma

Show them collectable cards of Hall of Famers. Most card shops have inexpensive cards of current or future Hall of Fame athletes. Hall of Fame recognition does make some cards very expensive (a Nolan Ryan rookie card is over $1,000). Show the children how statistics and other information are printed on the back of cards. The statistics tell what the athlete accomplished.

Did you know the Bible has a Hall of Fame? It's really a Hall of Faith, and you can read about it in Hebrews 11.

What is faith? Faith is being sure of what we hope for and certain of what we do not see.

Can you think of something we can not see, but we are certain exists? Can you name something we hope for and are sure we will receive? God. Heaven. Air. Love, etc.

We have faith (we're sure and certain) in God, Jesus, the Holy Spirit, and heaven even though we can not see them. Faith is important in pleasing God because without faith, we cannot believe God exists. It does not please God when people do not believe he exists. How would you feel if someone said you didn't exist or you weren't real?

On a second piece of paper, make a list of some or all of the names listed in Hebrews 11 by letting the kids try to guess the names, or give them clues to help them guess. You may tell the children that the names are from the Old Testament and let them guess from there or give them more hints for each name.

In the same way sports cards have statistics on the back, the book of Hebrews tells us a little about people in the Hall of Faith.

When they guess a name correctly, **"Why do you think that person is in the Hall of Faith? What did he or she do that took faith?"**

As you make the list, you may choose to tell some of the stories.

Abel	Adam and Eve's son, made sacrifices
Enoch	He did not die
Noah	The Ark
Abraham	Left home, offered Isaac
Sarah	Had a child in old age
Isaac	Father of Esau and Jacob
Jacob	Father of Joseph

Joseph	Instructions to take bones to Promised Land
Moses' Parents	Not afraid of the King
Moses	Led people out of Egypt, kept Passover
Israelites	Walls of Jericho fell down
Rahab	Helped the spies out of Jericho
Gideon	God's warrior
Barak	God's warrior
Samson	Strong
Jephthah	God's warrior
David	Killed Goliath
Samuel	Heard God's voice
Daniel	Shut the mouths of lions
Prophets	Spoke the word of God under persecution

These are people who pleased God because they believed in him. They showed that they believed in God when they did what he asked them to do.

◖ Application

If you have faith that God and heaven exist, then I want you to add your name to the Hall of Faith list.

Take a picture of each child. After the pictures are developed, another Family Time activity can be to decorate picture frames with the words, "Member of the Hall of Faith."

Lesson 9:
FIRM IN THE FAITH

TEACHING GOAL: Our surroundings can strengthen or weaken our faith.

1. Play theme song
2. Pray
3. Review last lesson
4. Lesson and discussion
5. Memorize: **Choosing wrong friends makes me weak; I become strong when God I seek.**
   or
   When choosing the wrong friends makes you squirm; choosing things of God will keep you firm.
6. Close in prayer

SCRIPTURE: 1 Corinthians 15:33 "Do not be misled: 'Bad company corrupts good character.'"

1 Corinthians 15:58 "Therefore, my dear brothers, stand firm. Let nothing move you. Always give yourselves fully to the work of the Lord, because you know that your labor in the Lord is not in vain."

Hebrews 10:25 "Let us not give up meeting together, as some are in the habit of doing, but let us encourage one another."

Ephesians 6:10 "Be strong in the Lord and in his mighty power."

MATERIALS: Paper and pen or pencil
Aluminum pie pan
Water
Cornstarch

Words that are written in **bold** are when you, the parent, are speaking. Feel free to use your own words.

▲ Big Idea

Whatever and whoever we surround ourselves with will impact us either for good or bad. God has called us to be strong in him (Ephesians 6:10). Satan wants to influence us, not because he loves us like God does, but because he hates God. Satan wants to keep us from God. We need to be careful of the kind of friends we choose and with whom we spend time. When our CLOSEST friends also love Jesus, their influence helps keep us strong. When we move away from those friends and their godly influence, we become spiritually weak. That's why it's important to go to church and spend time with friends who also attend church and believe in Jesus (Hebrews 10:25).

Ask the following questions:

Can you think of a time when someone influenced you to do something either good or bad?

Has anyone ever asked you to tell a lie? What if it was your very best friend? It's not easy to say no to someone who has become a very good friend.

Would a good friend who also knows lying is wrong, ask you to lie? It's not nearly as likely.

If you stayed up late on the night before church and you really wanted to sleep in, which person would make skipping church harder to do?

The friend who also goes to church and wants you to come too, or a friend who never goes to church and is also sleeping in? The one who wants you to go to church, too.

Can you think of other examples of a friend who keeps you strong and firm in making good choices? What about a friend who has made it hard for you to stand firm?

 **Activity**

PART 1: On your paper, make a list of things friends do to keep us strong and firm in Jesus. Make a second list of things that make us weak spiritually and move us away from a godly life. (Parents of younger children may want to do this ahead of time or do the writing themselves.)

EXAMPLE

Let's go to church today

Let's skip church and play videos instead.

Let's do our homework together.

I forgot to do my homework. Can I copy yours?

_____   _____

_____   _____

PART 2: On the fingertips of one hand, write initials of five Christian friends. On the fingertips of the other hand, draw symbols of the faith like the Bible, Holy Spirit (dove), church, and cross. Discuss the positive influence their Christian friends have on their lives. Then discuss the influence of church, the Bible, etc.

PART 3: Fill the pie pan with approximately $^1/_4$ cup of water and $^3/_4$ cup of cornstarch (or a 1:3 ratio). Mix. Mixture should be fairly thick. Have each person take turns reaching into the container, grabbing a handful of "glob," and squeezing it tightly in his or her fist.

Roll the "glob" into a ball and move it back and forth between your fingers. "Godly friends" and "things of God" are holding you firm. Stop rolling and moving the glob; release your grip and just let the mixture sit in your hands. Watch to see what happens. It will immediately begin to turn to its liquid form and become runny. Let children experiment with trying to keep it firm without holding it tightly or applying pressure. Allow time for children to enjoy the sensory experience and play as well.

◀ Application

How is this experiment like what we just talked about with friends? Our friends and things of God keep us strong. We take on the shape and remain firm in what we're around.

We need to surround ourselves with God's Word and God's people to stay strong. If we surround ourselves with those who don't love God we will grow weak in God and "hardened" in things that are opposed to God.

Lesson 10:
THE DOMINO EFFECT OF CHOICES

TEACHING GOAL: One person's choices may affect many other people in good and bad ways.

1. Play theme song
2. Pray
3. Review last lesson
4. Lesson and discussion
5. Memorize: **God is still there; when others' choices aren't fair.**
6. Close in prayer

SCRIPTURE: Genesis 15:1-5 God promises Abraham a son.

Genesis 16:1-15 Sarah (Sarai) still has not had a child and gives her maid, Hagar, to Abraham. Hagar conceives and problems begin between Sarai and Hagar, which leads to Hagar running away. God tells her to return and comforts her. Ishmael is born.

Genesis 17:18, 20 Abraham asks God to bless Ishmael and God promises He will bless him.

Genesis 21:1-21 Isaac is born to Sarah when Ishmael is 13 years old. More problems arise, leading to Hagar and Ishmael being sent away. God hears their cries and provides for them.

Genesis 25:8-9, 12-17 Abraham dies; Isaac and Ishmael bury him together. Ishmael has 12 sons and lives to be 137 years old.

MATERIALS: Set of dominoes

IN ADVANCE: You, and only you, as the parent should decide what the family will eat for dinner today. (If you go out, you will be the only one to decide where to go.)

Everyone must eat what you eat. As an added touch, serve something only you like for dinner, but for dessert, make it something your children especially like.

Words that are written in **bold** are when you, the parent, are speaking. Feel free to use your own words.

 Big Idea

Try to recall a time when your child played a team sport or participated in a group activity such as choir, band, or drama and a competition was lost or won because of one decision or one play (e.g. a tied soccer game and one child makes a goal in the last few seconds). Discuss how that one play affected the final result for the whole team, good or bad. **Have you ever had a teacher who made your whole class stay in for recess because a couple kids kept talking? Have you ever missed out on doing something you really wanted to do because it was cancelled?** Have children tell you about a time that they may have been disappointed or excited about something that happened as a result of someone else's actions or decisions.

Did you know that almost every decision we make affects others? Tonight I made the decision about where we were going to eat and didn't give you a choice. My decision affected you even though you had nothing to do with the choice. Sometimes this is good and sometimes this seems very unfair. When bad things happen because of choices other people make, it can affect us too.

B Activity

Set up the dominoes in the following way as you ask the "what if" questions below. Here is an example on how to use the "what if" scenarios. You will need to adapt your "what if" follow-up questions based on responses:

Set up a domino.

What if a person decides to drive after drinking too much alcohol?

He could kill someone in a car accident.

Set up a second domino next to the first so that they will both fall when the first domino is touched.

If the person who is killed is a man who is married, how will his wife feel?

Sad and alone.

Set up a third domino as above.

What if the man has a child, how will his child feel?

Also sad and lonely.

Keep going until you have ten or more dominoes set up. After the dominoes are set, knock the first one over and watch the chain reaction. **The chain reaction of the dominoes represents the chain reaction of our decisions.**

Let's answer some more "What if?" questions and think of some things that can happen as a result of one person's choices. Use both good and bad consequences to the "What if" choices. Help children think of scenarios for each action.

- **What if a child plays with matches and drops one accidentally?**
- **What if a lady throws a lit cigarette out of a car window in the forest?**
- **What if a family shares their extra car when a friend's car breaks down?**
- **What if a friend shares his lunch money with you when you forget yours?**

- What if someone vandalized your school so bad that it had to be closed down?
- What if a leader of a country decided to start a war?

Can you think of some of your own "What if" questions? Allow children to discuss things that may have happened to them as a result of decisions completely out of their control.

Did you notice how even the dominoes several places away from the first domino were also affected? That's the way it is for us as well. I might make a decision that affects you and then you do something that affects your friend, who then does something to affect his family.

Sometimes people make choices that affect us. Sometimes the effect is good and sometimes it's bad. The choices we make can affect other people too. I want to tell you a story about a boy and his family from the Bible. (Set up the dominoes again as you tell the story, adding a domino each time someone is affected by another person's choice.)

Tell the story of Abraham, Sarah, Hagar, and Ishmael in your own words, stressing how the choices of those around Ishmael affected him. (**NOTE TO PARENTS:** This may be a sensitive subject and your child may ask how it is that Abraham was married to Sarah yet had a child with Hagar. Customs were completely different during those times. It was an acceptable practice for men to have children with more than one wife as well as servants. It is no longer acceptable and even now seen as immoral, but Abraham was still a man of God and for his time in history, was not doing anything out of the ordinary. Your explanation will depend on the age of your child, but treat it with caution.)

Ishmael had to leave his father, the only home he had ever known, and move away because of someone else's decision. How do you think this made Ishmael feel? Sad and afraid. **The Bible says he cried as he wandered**

with his mother. Did Ishmael have anything to do with Sarah and Abraham having their own son Isaac? No. Hagar and Ishmael wandered in the desert and ran out of water. Hagar did not want to watch Ishmael die and she sobbed and Ishmael also cried. Have you ever cried because you were afraid? How did God provide for Hagar and her son? An angel came to her and God opened her eyes to see a well nearby. God promised to make Ishmael a great nation.

When bad things happen as a result of other people's decisions, does it mean that God no longer cares for us? No. **God still provided for Hagar and Ishmael and he still blessed Ishmael.**

Set up dominoes so that when the first one is tipped, all of them will fall over. Try this several times. Set up different patterns to see all the ways the dominoes fall. Allow children to set up and tip the dominoes.

DOMINO EFFECT OF CHOICES ON A FAMILY

Abraham wants a child. (Genesis 15)

God tells Abraham he will have a child. (Genesis 15)

Sarah, Abraham's wife, suggests Abraham have a child with her maidservant Hagar. (Genesis 16)

> **BAD CHOICE:** Resulting from Sarah and Abraham's lack of trust in God's promise.

Abraham accepts Sarah's offer and has a child with Hagar. (Genesis 16)

Hagar is about to have a baby and no longer likes Sarah. (Genesis 16)

Sarah treats Hagar badly. (Genesis 16)

> **BAD CHOICE:** Sarah is jealous of Hagar being pregnant.

Hagar runs away. (Genesis 16)

The Lord's angel finds Hagar in the desert and tells her to return. (Genesis 16)

Hagar goes back to Abraham and Sarah. (Genesis 16)

> **GOOD CHOICE:** Hagar obeys the Lord's angel.

Hagar gives birth to a baby boy and Abraham calls the boy Ishmael. (Genesis 16)

When Ishmael is 13 years old, God tells Abraham that Sarah will have a baby. Sarah is 90 and Abraham is 100. (Genesis 17)

> **GOOD CHOICE:** God chose to fulfill his promise of descendants as numerous as the stars.

Abraham and Sarah have a son they name Isaac. (Genesis 21)

Sarah gets upset with Hagar and Ishmael. (Genesis 21)

> **BAD CHOICE:** Sarah is jealous of Ishmael sharing the family's blessing.

Abraham sends Hagar and Ishmael away. (Genesis 21)

Hagar and Ishmael wander in the desert, run out of food, and lie down to die. (Genesis 21)

Angel of God rescues Hagar and blesses Ishmael; he will be a great nation. (Genesis 21)

Who was responsible for making the family decisions? Abraham.

Did Sarah have influence in family decisions? Sarah was too old to have a baby but was blessed with a son Isaac because of God's decision.

Did Hagar have influence in family decisions? Could Hagar have sent Sarah away? Hagar was sent away to the desert because someone else made a decision.

Did Ishmael have influence in family decisions? Ishmael almost died in the desert because someone else made a decision.

Others' decisions will have an impact on us. Our decisions will have an impact on others.

 **Application**

We must be very careful to think about each choice we make and how it might affect others. At the same time, realize that when some things happen to us, it may be a result of someone else's decision and no fault of our own.

Lesson 11:
DELAYED GRATIFICATION

TEACHING GOAL: Temporary discomfort can lead to greater rewards.

1. Play theme song
2. Pray
3. Review last lesson
4. Lesson and discussion
5. Memorize: **In heaven is my reward; when I'm sacrificing for my Lord.**
6. Close in prayer

SCRIPTURE: Matthew 6:19-21 "Do not store up for yourselves treasures on earth, where moth and rust destroy, and where thieves break in and steal. But store up for yourselves treasures in heaven, where moth and rust do not destroy, and where thieves do not break in and steal. For where your treasure is, there your heart will be also."

Matthew 5:11-12 "Blessed are you when people insult you, persecute you and falsely say all kinds of evil against you because of me. Rejoice and be glad, because great is your reward in heaven."

MATERIALS: Large bucket
      Water and ice
      20 marbles
      Dimes

IN ADVANCE: Fill the bucket with ice and water. You want the water to be very cold. Place marbles in the bottom of the bucket.

Words that are written in **bold** are when you, the parent, are speaking. Feel free to use your own words.

 Big Idea

Your willingness to put up with pain and discomfort to win a future reward is called "delayed gratification." Delayed gratification is a very important skill for Christians.

Jesus had a choice to die on the cross. He could have denied the responsibility of being the Son of God. But he went through the pain for the future reward of having Christians join with him in heaven.

Christians in other countries spend time in jail or suffer pain because they refuse to deny that they believe in Jesus. They do this because God has promised them a greater reward in heaven if they follow him on earth.

Because you are a Christian, friends may make fun of you. You may not be able to watch the same television shows as your friends. You may not be allowed to wear immodest clothes that are considered popular by your friends. When you give up something for Jesus, God promises that you will receive a greater reward when you get to heaven. Ask one person to read Matthew 6:19-21. Ask another person to read Matthew 5:11-12.

B Activity

There are 20 marbles in the bottom of the bucket. Take off one of your shoes and socks. I will give you a dime for every marble you pull out of the bucket with your toes. You can earn up to $2.00! You can only keep your foot out of the water for 5 seconds, just to pull out the marble. Give each child a turn.

Was keeping your foot in the water easier or harder than you expected? Listen. **Did the cold water hurt?** Listen. **Why would you keep your foot in the water even when the cold water hurt?** Listen. The reward of pulling out more marbles that were each worth a dime.

 **Application**

Ask participants to give examples of delayed gratification in their lives. If possible give an example that involves being a Christian.

- Going to church instead of sleeping late.
- Spending time memorizing scripture when your friends don't.
- Not watching a popular TV show because the violence or sexuality is dishonoring to God.
- Giving money to people who need to buy food instead of buying more candy or toys for yourself.

Lesson 12:
CHOCOLATE MILK

TEACHING GOAL: We need to let the Holy Spirit be our helper so that Jesus can be part of everything in our lives.

1. Play theme song
2. Pray
3. Review last lesson
4. Lesson and discussion
5. Memorize: **Holy Spirit, help me be true; to Jesus in everything I do.**
6. Close in prayer

SCRIPTURE: John 14:26 "But the Counselor, the Holy Spirit, whom the Father will send in my name, will teach you all things and will remind you of everything I have said to you."

John 15:26 "When the Counselor comes, whom I will send to you from the Father, the Spirit of truth who goes out from the Father, he will testify about me."

John 16:13 "But when he, the Spirit of truth, comes, he will guide you into all truth. He will not speak on his own; he will speak only what he hears, and he will tell you what is yet to come."

MATERIALS: Three clear glasses
Milk
Large heart cut out of cardboard
Chocolate syrup
Two spoons

Words that are written in **bold** are when you, the parent, are speaking. Feel free to use your own words.

 Big Idea

What are some things we've learned about the Holy Spirit? We can't see him. He helps us know whether something is right or not—that still, small voice we need to listen to.

The Bible has several verses about the Holy Spirit being our helper or counselor. Read the verses. **What things do we need help with?** Obeying Mom and Dad, being kind to other people, not losing my temper, being patient, etc.

 Activity

Place three glasses on the table. **These glasses each represent a different type of person.** Pour cold milk in each glass so it is 3/4 full. **The milk represents the choices we make in life like attitudes, thoughts, and actions.**

Put the cardboard heart over one of the glasses. **The opening of the glass represents the person's heart. We have three glasses, one represents a closed or hard heart and two are open. Jesus is the bottle of chocolate syrup. He is not welcome in the life of the person with a hard heart. Since the other two people have open hearts, Jesus can come in.** Pour in the chocolate syrup so that there is a visible layer of chocolate on the bottom of the glass.

These two people have Jesus in their lives. When we have Jesus we also have the Holy Spirit represented by this spoon. Place a spoon in each of the two glasses. Stir the spoon in one of the glasses and point out how the color of the milk changes. **The stirring represents the Holy Spirit**

being active in a person's life: listening to what the Spirit says and doing it. This person's life looks different. People can tell by the choices that he makes that he is a believer.

Do not stir the spoon in the other glass. **This represents the person who believes in Jesus, has the Holy Spirit in his life but does not listen to the Spirit or do what the Spirit says. The attitudes, thoughts, and actions (milk) looks a lot like the non-Christian. It's hard to see the difference. This might be a "Sunday Only" Christian.**

 # Application

The three glasses represent the three types of people in this world. The non-Christian who has a closed heart, the Christian who goes to church but doesn't let God influence his life, and the Christian who is actively listening to the Holy Spirit.

As a Christian have you got milk? Or have you got chocolate milk? Allow children to drink the milk and chocolate milk as you complete this lesson.

What would happen if the milk were frozen? Could we mix chocolate into it? No, because it would resist too much. **We don't want to be like frozen milk and not allow the Holy Spirit to work in our lives. We need to let the Holy Spirit help us be who Jesus wants us to be.**

What happens if we only stir a little and then quit stirring? The chocolate begins to settle back to the bottom. **It has more chocolate than before, but still not as much as it could if we kept stirring. So we always need to let the Holy Spirit help us because we don't want Jesus to settle back to the bottom of our lives. We want him to always be in every part of our lives.**

Lesson 13:
BLINDED BY SIN

TEACHING GOAL: Sin can blind us and lead to more sin in our lives.

1. Play theme song
2. Pray
3. Review last lesson
4. Lesson and discussion
5. Memorize: **When I can't see my sin; oh what trouble I'm in.**
6. Close in prayer

SCRIPTURE: 2 Corinthians 4:3-4 "And even if our gospel is veiled, it is veiled to those who are perishing. The god of this age has blinded the minds of unbelievers, so that they cannot see the light of the gospel of the glory of Christ, who is the image of God."

John 12:40 "He has blinded their eyes and deadened their hearts, so they can neither see with their eyes, nor understand with their hearts, nor turn—and I would heal them."

1 John 2:10-11 "Whoever loves his brother lives in the light, and there is nothing in him to make him stumble. But whoever hates his brother is in the darkness and walks around in the darkness; he does not know where he is going, because the darkness has blinded him."

MATERIALS: 2 bowls
1 cup uncooked white beans
1 cup uncooked black beans
3 cups uncooked red beans
(try to find beans of similar shape and size)
Blindfold

IN ADVANCE: Mix white, red, and black beans in a bowl.

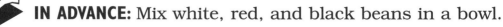

Words that are written in **bold** are when you, the parent, are speaking. Feel free to use your own words.

 **Big Idea**

When a blind person wants to go somewhere that he's never been before, how does he get there? He needs the help of a friend or guide. **Blind people today are very resourceful, using other senses to help them accomplish most anything. But because of blindness there are still a few things they can't do. Did you know that we can be blind spiritually? The Bible tells us that spiritual blindness means we may not understand that Jesus came to save us or we may not understand in our hearts when our words, actions, or behaviors are wrong.**

Just like the blind person needs help getting someplace new, we need God's help to overcome spiritual blindness. Spiritual blindness begins when we allow sin to become a regular part of our lives.

Read 1 John 2:10-11. **What does it mean to love your brother in the light?** Love your brother as Christ commands us. **Notice that the person who loves his brother does not stumble, he can see. What does it mean that the person who hates his brother can not see?** When we hate our brother we are not following Christ and we are blinded by our sin. **The person who hates his brother is lost in the dark.**

B **Activity**

Set the two bowls on the table. One is filled with the beans and the other is empty. **The bowl filled with beans represents all the choices we can make every day—choices in what we are going to do, say, and think. The black beans represent choices that are sin. The white beans represent choices that Jesus would want us to make. The red beans represent neutral decisions that may not be right or wrong. The empty second bowl**

represents our life. **Pick out ten white beans and put them in the second bowl.** Let every child have a turn. **Because you can see, you can avoid the black beans that represent sin. When you can see spiritually you can fill your life with good, godly choices in what you do, say, and think.**

Now, wearing a blindfold try the activity again and pick out ten white beans. Give each child a turn. **Select ten white beans and drop them into the second bowl.** When the child is finished, take the blindfold off. **Could you tell the difference between the white and black beans when you were blindfolded?** No. **In the same way, when we are spiritually blind—allowing sin in our lives—it is hard to choose what is right. Now that your blindfold has been removed, pick out the black or red beans and put them back in the other bowl.**

What kind of things do you think can blind us to God's ways? Listen to their answers. **Our verse for today gives us one example.** Read 1 John 2:10-11 again. **Did you ever think that not showing love to your brother or sister could blind you—like the blindfold—to what God wants you to do? Do you think this verse just means brothers and sisters in a family?** It means anyone, not just family. **God wants us to show love to everyone and when we fight with people, including brothers and sisters, it can blind you to what God wants us to do.**

Each day when we pray we need to ask God to show us the sin in our lives that we cannot see. God will help remove the spiritual blindness in our lives—the blindfold—so that we can see the sin and remove it from our lives. Parents, you may want to give an example of sin in your life that you didn't see until God took away your spiritual blindness.

◖ Application

Have the children and adults pray for God to remove spiritual blindness in your lives and to give you the ability to stop sinning and start making good choices.

Lesson 14:
SPIRITUAL COFFEE

 TEACHING GOAL: Christians are the fragrance of Christ in this world.

1. Play theme song
2. Pray
3. Review last lesson
4. Lesson and discussion
5. Memorize: **For Christ take a stance; to the world be a fragrance.**
6. Close in prayer

 SCRIPTURE: 2 Corinthians 2:15-16 "For we are to God the aroma of Christ among those who are being saved and those who are perishing. To the one we are the smell of death; to the other, the fragrance of life."

MATERIALS: Coffee maker, coffee filter
Coffee
OPTIONAL: Tea
3 film canisters or small containers numbered 1 to 3
3 cotton balls
3 scents: vanilla, bleach, coffee grounds (include one negative smell)

 IN ADVANCE: Put the scent on three cotton balls and place in containers. Put holes in the top of the containers so that participants can smell and guess the fragrances.

Words that are written in **bold** are when you, the parent, are speaking. Feel free to use your own words.

 **Big Idea**

Give each family member an opportunity to smell the fragrances in the containers and try to guess what the smell is. They can write down their guesses or report them to an adult who will write down their answers. Discuss their answers and include: **Were all the smells good?**

Christians are to be a fragrance in the world. What is a fragrance? Smell or scent. **Does a fragrance smell good or bad?** A fragrance can smell good or bad. Read 2 Corinthians 2:15-16. **We are to God the aroma of Christ among those who are being saved and those who are perishing. To the one we are the smell of death; to the other, the fragrance of life.**

The Bible says Christians are to be the fragrance of Christ. How can we smell like Christ? When we act like Christ or talk about Christ. **Why would we be the fragrance of life (good) to some people when we smell or act like Christ?** They can learn from us how to have eternal life in heaven. **Why would we be the fragrance of death** (bad) **to some people when we smell or act like Christ?** Some people do not like Christians and do not want to hear about Jesus. People might be doing things Jesus Christ tells us not to do and they don't want to stop doing what is wrong.

 **Activity**

I want you to help me make Spiritual Coffee. I'm going to make some first and then you can make some. You will need to remember what each element in Spiritual Coffee represents to make it correctly.

To make Spiritual Coffee you need to know the following:

> **God is the Power.**
> **Obedience is the Switch.**
> **Jesus is the Coffee.**
> **Our Heart is the Filter.**
> **The Holy Spirit is the Water.**
> **The Carafe is the World.**

Adapt the ingredients to match your coffee-making machine. You can also substitute tea.

Several things have to happen to generate the fragrance of coffee. Several things have to happen for us to be the fragrance of Christ, to be like Christ.

First, we need God. God is the power. Plug in the coffee maker.

Second, we need to be open to God's power. We need to be obedient so that God will be working in us. Flip the power switch.

Third, we need to have Jesus in our lives, in our heart. Put the coffee in the filter.

Fourth, God gave us the Holy Spirit to help us live like Jesus and to make our lives a witness to Christ. Pour the water into the coffee machine so that it will run through the coffee grounds and filter.

Fifth, the carafe is the world. When God is the power in our life, and when we are obedient and have Jesus in our hearts, and we add the work of the Holy Spirit, then we can be the fragrance of Christ in the world.

Give children an opportunity to make some coffee. They need to tell you what each element represents. BE SAFE. Do not let younger children near the power or hot coffee.

If appropriate, have a milk-coffee drink for a snack, coffee candy, or coffee ice cream.

 Application

The actions that we do help others see what kind of smell we have. When we do pleasant things like sharing, caring, giving, or loving, then we are smelling nice to others. But when we become selfish, angry, or rude, we start smelling bad. Those smells affect other people, so it's very important for us to choose our actions carefully.

Lesson 15:
BENT AND TORN

TEACHING GOAL: God is still with us and loves us when bad things happen.

1. Play theme song
2. Pray
3. Review last lesson
4. Lesson and discussion
5. Memorize: **Trust God to take the bad; and turn it into glad.**
6. Close in prayer

SCRIPTURE: 2 Corinthians 11:16-33 Paul's many trials and persecutions

2 Corinthians 12:10 "That is why, for Christ's sake, I delight in weaknesses, in insults, in hardships, in persecutions, in difficulties. For when I am weak, then I am strong."

2 Corinthians 4:8-9 "We are hard pressed on every side, but not crushed; perplexed, but not in despair; persecuted, but not abandoned; struck down, but not destroyed."

Romans 8:28 "And we know that in all things God works for the good of those who love him, who have been called according to his purpose."

MATERIALS: One 8 1/2″ x 11″ piece of paper
Pen or pencil

Words that are written in **bold** are when you, the parent, are speaking. Feel free to use your own words.

 Big Idea

Have you ever had anything bad happen to you? Have you ever been sick or hurt? Everyone has occasional unpleasant experiences. Some people blame God when these times occur, but we shouldn't. God loves us and doesn't enjoy seeing us hurt, but we live in a world where bad things happen. When they do, God can use them to help us grow stronger.

 Activity

Read through 2 Corinthians 11:16-33 and make a list of all the things that happened to Paul. Discuss the many things that happened. **How would you react if someone threw rocks at you for telling about Jesus? How would you react if you were shipwrecked? Beaten? Whipped? Let's look and see what Paul's reaction was.** Read 2 Corinthians 12:10 for Paul's reaction. **Was Paul angry or bitter at God? Why not?**

Tell me about some bad things that have happened to you in your life. Add your examples to Paul's list. **Do you think God still cared for you even when those things happened?**

Turn the paper over and start a list of how God uses bad times in the life of Paul to accomplish good things:

> Paul was blinded on the road to Damascus...
> > ...that is how Paul met Jesus.
> Paul put up with hard travel from country to country...
> > ...the Gentiles learned about Jesus from Paul.
> Paul was thrown in prison...
> > ...the prison guards learned about Jesus.
> Paul was on trial before Caesar...
> > ...the Roman government heard about Jesus.

Add to the list examples of how God has taken bad times in your life and made them into something good.

Read 2 Corinthians 4:8-9. (See diagram.) Using an 8¹/2″ x 11″ piece of paper, fold the right upper corner down to the left edge. (With each fold discuss how we are often bent, folded, and crushed. Push down...press...and crush with each fold, referring to the verse.) Fold the left top pointed edge down, matching the lower edge of your previous fold, forming a peak. Fold paper in half from left to right. The left edge will be straight and the right edge will be angled. (See next page for diagram.)

Fold over the shorter diagonal edge back toward the long edge so that it touches or overlaps some. Open this fold back up and tear along the fold. Read Romans 8:28.

 **Application**

Even when bad things happen to us, God knows and loves us. We don't always understand, but God does and will help us. Open up the paper. **This sheet of paper was folded, bent, crushed, and torn, but look what happened. What is it now?** A cross. **God has a plan and purpose for our lives, even when bad things happen. We can trust in God and his love for us.**

BENT AND TORN DIAGRAM

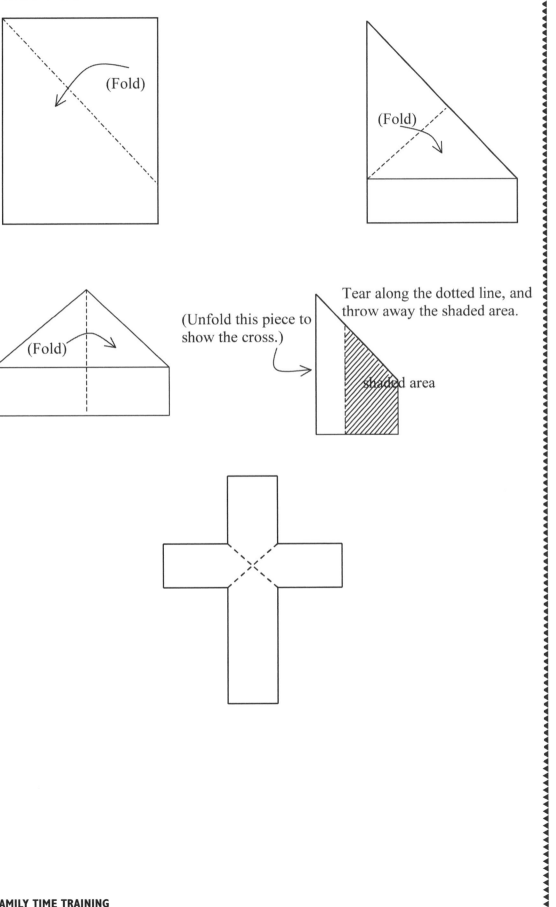

(Fold)

(Fold)

(Fold)

(Unfold this piece to show the cross.)

Tear along the dotted line, and throw away the shaded area.

shaded area

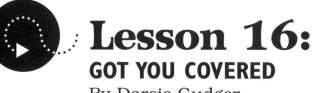

Lesson 16:
GOT YOU COVERED
By Darcie Gudger

 TEACHING GOAL: Jesus' sacrifice on the cross covers our sin.

1. Play theme song
2. Pray
3. Review last lesson
4. Lesson and discussion
5. Memorize: **When God looks in; he sees Jesus not my sin.**
6. Close in prayer

 SCRIPTURE: Genesis 1:26 "Then God said, 'Let us make man in our image, in our likeness.'"

2 Corinthians 5:17 "Therefore, if anyone is in Christ, he is a new creation; the old has gone, the new has come!"

 **MATERIALS:** 1 sheet of pastel color paper for each person
1 sheet of white paper for each person
Colored pencils, crayons, or markers
Glue, scissors
Child's favorite ice cream or other treat

Words that are written in **bold** are when you, the parent, are speaking. Feel free to use your own words.

Big Idea

Understanding the work of Christ is not just a theological concept. It's very practical for the development of self-concept in children. Sometimes guilt can rob kids of confidence and a positive view of life. Certainly when they've done something wrong they need to confess it and deal with it. But sometimes kids view themselves as inadequate and lacking worth.

The sacrifice of Christ provides a beautiful way for us to accept his forgiveness and rely on his grace. When we acknowledge Jesus as Lord, then we rely on his goodness and not our own. You'll have opportunity in this lesson to teach your children some valuable things about this truth.

B▶ Activity

Read Genesis 1:26. **We are made in the image of God. God made us with some of the same characteristics that he has. God is a creator, we can create. God is love, we can love. Can you think of other God characteristics we share?** Listen to answers. Giving, patient, appreciation of beauty. **Can you think of some God characteristics we don't share?** Listen to answers. All-powerful. All-knowing. Eternal. Holy—without sin.

Take the colored piece of paper and fold it in half so it looks like a book. Help younger children fold the paper. **On the cover of your book, write your name at the top and draw a picture of yourself under your name.**

Open up your book and you will see there are two pages separated by a crease. On the top of the left-side page write, "God's Image." Draw pictures or make a list of things that you have in common with God.

IDEAS: Draw a heart to represent love. Draw a hammer to represent creating. Draw a sunset to represent beauty. Draw two friends together to represent friendship. Draw a smiley face to represent happiness.

On the top of the right-side page write, "Sin." God is perfect and we are imperfect. God is always right, we are sometimes wrong. God is holy and we sin. Draw pictures or make a list of sins.

IDEAS: Draw a mean and angry face. Draw a fist to represent hitting. Draw a mouth that is yelling to represent bad words. Write "NO" in big letters to represent disobedience.

Close the book. Now pretend you are God looking at the front cover of the book. You see (child's name). Open up the book. You know everything about this person. You know the good and the bad. Close the book again and set it to the side.

Everyone needs a half-sheet of white paper. Fold the white paper like a book and cut along the crease. Give each person a half-sheet of white paper. **This white paper represents Jesus. You can write the name "Jesus" in big letters on the white piece of paper, or you can draw a cross to represent Jesus, or you can draw your own picture of Jesus on the paper.** Give everyone time to write or draw on the white half-sheet of paper.

Ask each person to open up their color-paper book. **Jesus died on the cross for our sins. Our sins disappear when we believe and accept Jesus' sacrifice on the cross. Glue the picture of Jesus over the right-side page. In the same way Jesus is now in our book, Jesus wants to come into our lives.**

Close the book. Again, pretend that you are God looking at the front cover of the book. You see (child's name). Open the book. You see those things made in God's image and you no longer look at the sin. You see Jesus, your son who died for (child's name)'s sin.

 **Application**

When I look at you I see Jesus. That means I want to value you and treasure you. You are a special person to me. I know that we have to get family business done and so I rush you here, or require that you help out there. Sometimes I even have to correct you, but I want you to know that you are a treasure to me. God gave you to me and you're special.

We all need to think about each other that way. Sometimes because of the work of family life, we get distracted from that reality. Let's work on valuing each other this week. In fact, to value you I've picked some great ice cream for us to enjoy this evening.

Lesson 17:
PLUMB LINE

TEACHING GOAL: As we build our lives, Christ is our foundation and scripture is our "plumb line."

1. Play theme song
2. Pray
3. Review last lesson
4. Lesson and discussion
5. Memorize: **If we use God's rules of thumb; then our lives will line up plumb.**
6. Close in prayer

SCRIPTURE: Amos 7:7-8 "This is what he showed me: The Lord was standing by a wall that had been built true to plumb, with a plumb line in his hand. And the LORD asked me, 'What do you see, Amos?' 'A plumb line,' I replied. Then the Lord said, 'Look, I am setting a plumb line among my people Israel; I will spare them no longer.'"

Isaiah 28:16-17 "This is what the Sovereign LORD says: 'See, I lay a stone in Zion, a tested stone, a precious cornerstone for a sure foundation; the one who trusts will never be dismayed. I will make justice the measuring line and righteousness the plumb line.'"

2 Timothy 3:16 "All Scripture is God-breathed and is useful for teaching, rebuking, correcting and training in righteousness."

MATERIALS: Level
String
Heavy washer or weight to tie on string to use as a plumb line
Paper and marker
Large piece of paper (flip chart or butcher block paper works well)
Sticky notes or small square papers with tape on the back

Small building blocks (the Jenga game works well if you stack them on the sides, or square baby blocks or legos stacked on the sides) *You will need just enough blocks that the kids can make a tower that won't fall over.*

 IN ADVANCE: Test out the games in advance and prepare a large piece of paper by drawing several parallel lines across the paper. Draw the lines at a slight angle so that they are not perpendicular to the sides of the paper. Tape the piece of paper on the wall also at a slight angle. Draw several "X's" on the paper away from the edges.

Words that are written in **bold** are when you, the parent, are speaking. Feel free to use your own words.

 Big Idea

We are going to learn about two important tools used in building. The first is called a level. The level measures when something is flat or tilted. (Show them a level and let them practice using it.) **The second tool is a plumb line. The plumb line helps us measure straight up and down.** (Show them a plumb line and let them practice using it.)

There is a book in the Bible about a man named Amos. Amos was a shepherd. Can you think of other shepherds in the Bible? David. The shepherds who came to see the baby Jesus. **God gave Amos visions, like dreams, about things that are going to happen. One of the visions was about a plumb line** (Amos 7:7-8):

The Lord was standing by a vertical wall, with a plumb line in his hand. And the Lord said to me, "What do you see, Amos?" And I said, "A plumb line."

Then the Lord said, "Behold I am about to put a plumb line in the midst of my people Israel. I will spare them no longer."

The Israelites were not following God's commandments. They were worshipping idols. God's commandments are the plumb line, and when he measured the Israelites' actions against his commandments, they didn't line up. This did not please God.

B Activity

Ask the kids to hang sticky notes on each of the four "X's" and try to hang them level by themselves.

The large piece of paper represents being human. All of us have sinned; we've all done things that are wrong. That is why the paper is hung at an angle and not straight.

The slanted lines represent the culture in which we live. There are things that are legal, but are not right for Christians to do. That is why the lines are not straight across the paper. An example might be that there are lots of movies we can watch, but God does not want us to watch all the fighting, immodest behavior, and bad language in some movies.

The sticky notes represent our actions. Even when we want to do what is right (like trying to hang the notes straight), it can be really difficult because of the influences of our sinful natures and culture.

Use an example relevant to your kids: language, friends, obedience, TV shows, or movies.

After each child has had a chance to put the sticky notes on the "X's" and you have explained what the parts mean, let the children put the sticky notes on again using the plumb line. **The plumb line represents God's Word, his commandments. If we follow God's directions, then our actions will line up with God's directions.**

God gave us Jesus to be the cornerstone of our life. If we follow Jesus and do what he says, then our lives will be built on a firm foundation. A cornerstone is the most important stone in a building. It is very strong and solid. It is part of the foundation. When building a structure, if the cornerstone is weak or placed wrong, the whole structure will be weak and unstable. Jesus is the cornerstone for our lives. If we build our lives on him, then we will be strong in the faith and stable. If he is not our cornerstone, then our lives will be weak and unstable.

Use the level to see if the blocks are flat. Have the children see if they can stack all the blocks into a stable tower. **With a solid, level foundation we can build a tall tower. With Jesus as**

our foundation in life, our activities will be good and sturdy.

Now take five (or ten) pieces of paper and put the bottom block half on and half off of the stack of paper. Talk with the children about how when the foundation is not level, even a little bit, you cannot build a straight high tower. **When Jesus is not our foundation, then what we do in life will crash.**

◖► Application

There is a right way and a wrong way to build a house. If you build it the wrong way you will have an unsturdy house that will fall down. If you build it the right way, it will be strong and sturdy for a long time. In the same way, you can have a strong, healthy life by obeying God and keeping his commands.

Lesson 18:
THE COMPANY WE KEEP

TEACHING GOAL: Be careful whom you hang around with because bad influences affect you.

1. Play theme song
2. Pray
3. Review last lesson
4. Lesson and discussion
5. Memorize: **God's approval I'll seek; in the friends I keep.**
6. Close in prayer

SCRIPTURE: 1 Corinthians 15:33 "Do not be misled: 'Bad company corrupts good character.'"

Matthew 16:6 "'Be careful,' Jesus said to them. 'Be on your guard against the yeast of the Pharisees and Sadducees.'"

2 Corinthians 6:14, 17 "Do not be yoked together with unbelievers. For what do righteousness and wickedness have in common? Or what fellowship can light have with darkness? 'Therefore come out from them and be separate.'"

MATERIALS: Two clear glasses
Pitcher of water
Approximately 1/2 cup of dirt
Spoon or something to stir with
2 small round magnets

Words that are written in **bold** are when you, the parent, are speaking. Feel free to use your own words.

 **Big Idea**

Have you ever had a friend ask you to do something with them? Of course! Friends like to do things together. Spending time with a special friend, sharing interests, and making memories is important to friends and makes you closer. What if your friends wanted you to do something that you knew was very wrong? Hanging around people who do bad things could lead you to sharing interests with them that could get you into trouble.

The Bible warns us about becoming friends with these people. 1 Corinthians 15:33 says "Do not be misled: 'Bad company corrupts good character.'" What does this mean? Give children an opportunity to explain and give examples of people they may know that had this happen to them. **Be very careful about who you choose to be your closest friends. A little bit of the wrong influence can have a big effect on you.**

B **Activity**

As the children watch, pour some water into both of the glasses. Put dirt in one glass and stir it to mix completely. You will now have a glass of clean water and a glass of muddy water. Hold glass of clean water out to children. **Would you like a sip of this water?** Take a sip yourself if child doesn't want a drink. Now offer the glass of muddy water. **Would you drink from this glass? Why not?** It's dirty and could make us sick. Pour a small amount of the muddy water into the clean water. **Would you drink from this glass now?** No, it's dirty too. **But I only put a very small amount of dirty water in the clean water. It's not that dirty. Why won't you drink it?** It's still dirty, even if it's only a small amount of dirt. **That's the way it is with hanging around people with the wrong influence.**

It doesn't take very much to begin to influence us. We need to keep good company so that we can stay clean ourselves. Empty the glass but do not clean it, and refill with clean water. **Will you take a drink now? Is it clean enough?** Glass is probably still dirty and children will want to see it cleaned further.

We can clean ourselves (empty glass and clean it out) **of the old influences by asking forgiveness and asking God to make us clean again** (refill clean glass with clean water). **Will you take a drink now? Is it clean enough?** Yes.

The Pharisees and Sadducees went to church regularly, but Jesus warns us that just going to church doesn't always make a person a good influence. Have you ever known anyone at church who influenced you in a negative way?

The Bible warns in Matthew 16:6: "Be careful," Jesus said to them. "Be on your guard against the yeast of the Pharisees and Sadducees." Yeast is the ingredient put in bread that makes it rise. It only takes a small amount to make the dough grow. What do you think Jesus meant when he said this? A little bit of yeast makes the whole lump of dough rise and a little bit of the wrong influence can go a long way. The Pharisees and Sadducees were very religious but their hearts weren't right. They didn't really love God. **We need to keep our eyes on Jesus and our relationships based on him and what he would want. When we seek his will in even our friendships, he will protect us from influences that could hurt us.**

Lay magnets on a flat surface near each other. **God wants us to be a positive influence and draw people to us, just as these magnets attract each other.** Move magnets close enough so that they begin to pull each other closer together.

We need to be around people who don't know God so that they will want to know more. However, it's just as important that we don't attach ourselves to certain people whose influence will pull us away from God. Turn magnets so that they are "repelling" each other and let children feel the force that is pushing them apart. **Our very closest friends should be the ones who also love God and want his will for their lives too.**

 ## Application

Have you ever heard the word yoke? To be "yoked" is to be attached together. 2 Corinthians 6:14 warns us not to be yoked together with unbelievers but to be separate. Turn magnets so that they attract each other. **Just as these magnets attract each other, we should attract and stick with those who will not turn us from God. While it's important to not separate ourselves so completely that we no longer influence others who don't know Jesus** (lay magnets side by side again), **we need to remember to flee from those who will hurt our relationship with Jesus** (hold magnets again so that they repel each other).

Lesson 19:
ROCKS CRY OUT

TEACHING GOAL: All creation praises God.

1. Play theme song
2. Pray
3. Review last lesson
4. Lesson and discussion
5. Memorize: **To God cry out; or the rocks will shout.**
6. Close in prayer

SCRIPTURE: Luke 19:40 "'I tell you,' he replied, 'if they keep quiet, the stones will cry out.'"

Hebrews 13:15 "Through Jesus, therefore, let us continually offer to God a sacrifice of praise—the fruit of lips that confess his name."

MATERIALS: 24 round, flat stones approximately 2″ in diameter
Permanent marker

Words that are written in **bold** are when you, the parent, are speaking. Feel free to use your own words.

 **Big Idea**

"The Triumphal Entry" is a phrase used to describe the day that Jesus came back to Jerusalem. He rode into Jerusalem on the back of a donkey while a crowd of people yelled "Hosanna" and "Blessed is the king who comes in the name of the Lord!" There were some people in the crowd that didn't like Jesus. They didn't believe that Jesus was the Son of God. They told Jesus to make the people stop shouting praises. Listen to what Jesus said. Read Luke 19:40. **He said that if the people kept quiet then the rocks would cry out.**

B▶ Activity

As a family, go to a river bed or rock pile and find 24 round, flat stones. The flatter the stones the better. You may want to go to a garden center and purchase the stones.

There are several places in the Bible that talk about creation praising God. What do you think the rocks would say? They would probably say what we are supposed to say when we praise God. Make a list of their answers. Here are some ideas:

Hosanna	Lord	Glory	Honor
Holy	Hallelujah	Prince of Peace	King of Kings
Righteous	Creator	Savior	Thank you

We have twenty-four rocks. We are going to write 11 words of praise on two rocks each. On the last two rocks we will write "Alpha and Omega" which means God is the first and the last.

After you write the words on the 24 rocks, turn them over and mix them up. Take turns playing the matching game. Try to turn over two rocks with the same word. Players get one point for each match with the exception of 2 points for matching the "Alpha" rock with the "Omega" rock. The player with the most points wins.

C▶ Application

It's funny to think about rocks crying out or creation praising God. But the reality is that we can see God in the things he has made. In the spring or fall the trees change color. In the winter, beautiful snow covers mountains. Thunder and rain reveal God's blessing and awesome power.

Our job is to praise God. It's interesting to think that if we didn't do our job that God would give mouths to creation to offer praise to him.

Lesson 20:
PRAYING CONTINUALLY

TEACHING GOAL: We can talk to God anytime.

1. Play theme song
2. Pray
3. Review last lesson
4. Lesson and discussion
5. Memorize: **I can talk to God any time of day; in my mind or out loud, either's okay.**
6. Close in prayer
   Lead children in a silent prayer:
   - Ask them to pray for a friend silently—silence as they pray.
   - Have them thank God for something—silence.
   - Ask God for something—silence.
   - Say Amen.

Afterwards, ask them who and what they prayed for during the silence. Reinforce that God hears all our prayers, even those not spoken out loud.

SCRIPTURE: 1 Samuel 1 Story of Hannah asking for a son and having her request answered.

1 Samuel 1:12-13 "As she kept on praying to the LORD, Eli observed her mouth. Hannah was praying in her heart, and her lips were moving but her voice was not heard."

1 Thessalonians 5:17 "Pray continually."

Ephesians 6:18 "And pray in the Spirit on all occasions with all kinds of prayers and requests. With this in mind, be alert and always keep on praying for all the saints."

MATERIALS: Paper and pencil

Words that are written in **bold** are when you, the parent, are speaking. Feel free to use your own words.

Big Idea

God instructs us to pray without ceasing. That idea can be confusing. In this lesson you will explore different ways to communicate and apply those communication ideas to prayer.

Activity

As children join you, tap one on the shoulder and point to the paper and pencil, which should be left nearby, making a motion to bring it to you. Do not speak out loud. Make your gestures simple, not drawing attention to what you are doing.

I want you to add two numbers together. Tell them the numbers, choosing the numbers based on the age and skill of the children so that adding can be done easily in their heads. **How did you do that?** I did it in my head. **Using the paper and pencil write down the numbers and add them.** For younger children, you may want to count out slash marks and count them all to show the process of adding the two numbers together. **Explain to me how you did this in your head.** I was able to picture it in my mind and add it together forming the answer. (If children are younger they may need help with the idea of picturing it in their minds and initially say, "I don't know.")

We can think in our minds. We can also communicate to others without actually forming and speaking words out loud. When I gestured for you to get me the paper and pencil did I speak out loud? No. **Did you understand and respond even though I did not speak out loud?** Yes.

In the same way that we can do math in our heads or communicate with others without using words, we can pray in our heads and communicate with God. The Bible tells us in 1 Thessalonians 5:17 to pray continually. Read Ephesians 6:18 too. **How can we do this?** By praying in our heads whenever we think about it.

In your own words, tell the story of Hannah from 1 Samuel 1. **Hannah wasn't speaking out loud but did God still hear her?** Yes. **How do we know?** The Bible tells us that he heard. In this case he answered her prayer by giving her a son. Even if he hadn't given her the son, we know he still heard her prayer. **God hears us even when we don't pray out loud.**

Take turns lip-reading simple sentences such as "come here" or "I love you" and making simple gestures (i.e. smile, a nod of the head) to communicate what you are thinking. **We are able to communicate without using words.**

Sometimes when we are in a crowded room and cannot speak, we can still make contact and communicate with lip-reading or gestures. If you see me across a crowded room and I motion for you to come and mouth the words "let's go," you know what I mean, don't you? We can still communicate or pray even when we are busy or others are around, by praying in our heads. God wants us to talk to him all day long. He wants us to tell him about what we are doing and wants us to talk to him about the people we come in contact with during the day. We can do this anytime during the day, in our heads.

▶ Application

Teach your children "the family squeeze":
Tell them that anytime you squeeze their hand or tap them (or do anything) in a series of three, that you are communicating to them a special message without using words. You are telling them I (1) LOVE (2) YOU (3)! Use this in the future to let them know you love them and as a reminder that we don't always need spoken words to communicate.

OPTIONAL: Play a simple game of charades to reinforce communicating without speaking out loud.

Lesson 21:
AMBASSADOR

 TEACHING GOAL: As a Christian, you represent Christ to non-Christians.

1. Play theme song
2. Pray
3. Review last lesson
4. Lesson and discussion
5. Memorize: **I am Christ's Ambassador to my neighbor.**
6. Close in prayer

 SCRIPTURE: Ephesians 6:19-20 "Pray also for me, that whenever I open my mouth, words may be given me so that I will fearlessly make known the mystery of the gospel, for which I am an ambassador in chains."

2 Corinthians 5:20 "We are therefore Christ's ambassadors, as though God were making his appeal through us."

John 3:16 "For God so loved the world that he gave his one and only Son, that whoever believes in him shall not perish but have eternal life."

 MATERIALS: Paper and markers
Prize (balloon, sticker, etc.)
Ambassador Description forms

IN ADVANCE: This lesson is best done with another family or two. In advance tell others about your Family Time experience and invite them to join in with you for an evening. Not only will your friends enjoy having Family Time, but they may catch a vision for having their own regular Family Times too.

Words that are written in **bold** are when you, the parent, are speaking. Feel free to use your own words.

◤ Big Idea

On the top of a piece of paper write WHO ARE YOU? Let the children and adults throw out answers to the question. Answers may include: names, nicknames, things they do (athlete, soccer player, student), character qualities (quiet, funny, compassionate, Christian). Give suggestions if necessary, but fill the paper.

This page is filled with our given names, things we do, and character qualities. Now we are going to look at who God says we are.

On the top of another piece of paper write WHO ARE YOU? Underneath write the word "Ambassador." **In a letter to a group of people called Corinthians, the Bible says we are ambassadors for Christ.**

What is an ambassador? Let them guess or answer. **Our country sends ambassadors to other countries. We have an ambassador who lives in Mexico. This ambassador learns about the Mexican people and tells them about the American people.**

◤ Activity

Divide into a minimum of three groups (this is a great multiple family activity). Each group includes children and adults. Give each group a copy of the "Ambassador Description" form. Groups work together to fill out the "yours" section of the form to create their own make-believe country. The group comes up with a name for their country, the continent on which it is located, national animal, etc.

Number the groups. When they have filled out the section titled "yours," then have two ambassadors (adult and child) go from group 1 to group 2. The ambassadors from group 1 tell group 2 about their country and then they write down on the group 1 form under "theirs" what they learn from group 2. Group 2 does not write anything about group 1 on their Ambassador form because they are not acting as ambassadors yet. Then group 2 sends two ambassadors to group 3. The last group sends ambassadors to group 1.

After every group has had a turn, ask again, **"What is an ambassador?"** Now the kids will understand how an ambassador goes to another country to learn about the other country and tells about his country.

◖▶ Application

What do you think the Bible means when it says we are Christ's ambassadors? Let them guess or answer the question. **There are two groups of people in the world: Christians and non-Christians. As Christians, we represent Christ to non-Christians. We are Christ's ambassadors to non-Christians who do not have a relationship with Jesus.**

As Christ's ambassadors, there are five things we need to tell non-Christians:

1. **God loves you.**
2. **God sent his son Jesus.**
3. **Jesus died for you.**
4. **Believe in Jesus and be saved.**
5. **Live for Jesus.**

God sends the Holy Spirit to prepare people to hear the message from Christ's ambassadors. There are three types of responses we will get from people when we tell them these five points.

1. **Some will be interested and may want to hear more. The Holy Spirit has prepared their hearts to hear the message.**

2. Some will be confused and what we say won't make sense to them.

3. Some will not be interested and may even be angry.

Only those people whom the Holy Spirit has prepared in advance will be ready to hear the message. Share with those who want to hear, and don't force the message on those who do not want to hear.

Now have one adult go into another room to represent a non-Christian who does not know about Jesus. The kids practice memorizing the five points with the other adults. One at a time as each child memorizes the five points, he or she goes into the other room and shares the points with the adult who represents the non-Christian. Then they receive a special prize.

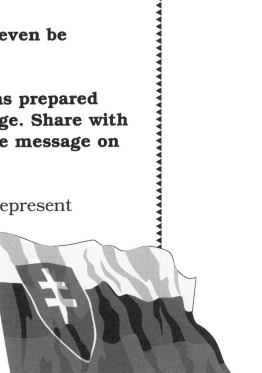

AMBASSADOR DESCRIPTION

	Yours	Theirs
Name of Country:	_____	_____
Continent:	_____	_____
National Animal:	_____	_____
National Flower:	_____	_____
Type of Land:	mountains, forests, deserts, ice	mountains, forests, deserts, ice
	(Circle One)	(Circle One)
Closest Ocean:	_____	_____
National Song:	_____	_____
3 Flag Colors:	_____	_____
Describe the people who live in your country.	_____ _____ _____	_____ _____ _____

Index

Seeing is Believing (ALL AGES)

1: Build Your House on the Rock..Matthew 7:24-27
2: Our Value..Romans 5:8, John 3:16, Psalm 8:5-7
3: The Trinity..Mark 1:10-11, Matthew 28:19
4: Traps..Joshua 23:12-13
5: Doubting Thomas..John 20:24-29
6: Take Out the Garbage..2 Corinthians 2:14-15, Deuteronomy 5:7-21, 2 Corinthians 12:20, 2 Corinthians 4:2, Galatians 5:20-23, Matthew 15:19
7: Spiritual Memory Inventory..Deuteronomy 6:5-9
8: Make Time for Rest..Genesis 2:2, Exodus 20:8, Matthew 14:23, Ecclesiastes 4:6, Psalm 46:10, Psalm 51:10
9: Three Brave Friends..Daniel 1, Daniel 3
10: Seeing Scripture..Ephesians 3:17-18, Colossians 2:6-7
11: Promise Keepers..Psalm 33:4, Deuteronomy 31:6, John 14:26, Acts 2:21, John 14:2-3, Titus 1:2, Proverbs 3:5-6, 2 Chronicles 7:14, Galatians 5:22-23
12: Pray for the President..Romans 13:1-2, 1 Timothy 2:1-2, 2 Chronicles 7:14
13: Peer Pressure..Proverbs 1:8-10
14: Christmas Future..Isaiah 9:6, Isaiah 7:14, Micah 5:2
15: Chains..Ephesians 6:19-20, Colossians 4:18
16: Web of Love..Matthew 22:39, Matthew 5:44, John 13:35
17: Knock Sin Out of Our Lives..Romans 3:23, Hebrews 4:15, 1 John 5:17
18: Creation..Genesis 1:1, Genesis 1, Romans 1:20, Colossians 1:16-17
19: Tithe..Leviticus 27:30, Malachi 3:10
20: Holy Spirit and the Glove..Acts 1:8, Philippians 2:12-13, Hebrews 13:20-21
21: Book of Life..Revelation 20:15, 21:27

Playing for Keeps (ALL AGES)

1: Scripture Cake..Matthew 4:4, John 4:34
2: Modesty..Genesis 2:21 to 3:11
3: Lukewarm Spit..Revelation 3:15-16
4: Dem Bones..Ezekiel 37:1-14
5: Relationship with God..Genesis 3, Romans 3:23, John 3:16-17
6: Obedience..Ephesians 6:1, Romans 6:17, Genesis 18:19
7: Repentance..Acts 26:20, Acts 9, Jonah 2, 2 Kings 22-23
8: The Hall of Faith..Hebrews 11:6, Hebrews 11:1, Hebrews 11
9: Firm in the Faith..1 Corinthians 15:33, 1 Corinthians 15:58, Hebrews 10:25, Ephesians 6:10
10: The Domino Effect of Choices..Genesis 15:1-5, Genesis 16:1-15, Genesis 17:18, 20, Genesis 21:1-21, Genesis 25:8-9, 12-17
11: Delayed Gratification..Matthew 6:19-21, Matthew 5:11-12
12: Chocolate Milk..John 14:26, John 15:26, John 16:13
13: Blinded by Sin..2 Corinthians 4:3-4, John 12:40, 1 John 2:10-11
14: Spiritual Coffee..2 Corinthians 2:15-16
15: Bent and Torn..2 Corinthians 11:16-33, 2 Corinthians 12:10, 2 Corinthians 4:8-9, Romans 8:28
16: Got You Covered..Genesis 1:26, 2 Corinthians 5:17
17: Plumb Line..Amos 7:7-8, Isaiah 28:16-17, 2 Timothy 3:16
18: The Company We Keep..1 Corinthians 15:33, Matthew 16:6, 2 Corinthians 6:14, 17
19: Rocks Cry Out..Luke 19:40, Hebrews 13:15
20: Praying Continually..1 Samuel 1, 1 Samuel 1:12-13, 1 Thessalonians 5:17, Ephesians 6:18
21: Ambassador..Ephesians 6:19-20, 2 Corinthians 5:20, John 3:16

Running the Race (ALL AGES)

1: God's Word—The Sword for Battle..Ephesians 6:10-18, Matthew 4:1-11
2: Mission Mail..Matthew 28:19-20, Acts 1:8, 2 Corinthians 8:3-5, Colossians 4:3-4
3: Mirror..James 1:22-25
4: Josiah..2 Kings 22 to 2 Kings 23:30
5: Jeshua..Zechariah 3:1-2, Zechariah 10:4, Luke 22:31-32
6: Holy Spirit Guide..John 14:26, John 16:13
7: Halloween: Choose Your Attitude..2 Corinthians 11:23-27, Philippians 4:11-13
8: Mold Me..Jeremiah 18:1-6, Acts 2:37, Romans 12:2, Proverbs 4:14, 1 Thessalonians 5:11
9: God's Protection..Psalm 91:11-12
10: God-Given Differences..Matthew 8:1-3, Matthew 9:29-30, Matthew 9:9-10, Matthew 15:21-22, Matthew 19:13-14
11: Anger..Psalm 37:7-8, Colossians 3:8, 12
12: God Uses Our Abilities..Exodus 31:3, Exodus 31:1-11
13: Family Mentors..Deuteronomy 4:9, 2 Timothy 1:5, Esther 2:7
14: Eternity..Romans 6:22, Galatians 6:8
15: Forgiven Sins Disappear..Psalm 103:12, Romans 5:8, Colossians 2:13-14, Romans 3:23, Romans 6:23
16: Don't Schedule Jesus Out..Luke 10:38-42
17: Added Value..Luke 15:11-32, 1 Peter 2:9
18: Prayer Cube..Matthew 6:9-13, Ephesians 6:18
19: God's Direction For Our Lives..2 Timothy 3:16-17
20: Hitting the Target..Psalm 119:9-11, Romans 8:26-27, 1 Peter 2:21-22

Wiggles, Giggles, & Popcorn (PRESCHOOLERS)

1: Noah's Ark..Genesis 6:14-16
2: Moses..Exodus 2:3
3: Ruth..Book of Ruth
4: Priscilla and Aquila—The Gift of Hospitality..Acts 18:1-2, 1 Corinthians 16:19, 1 Peter 4:9

Index

5: **Soak It Up!** ....Psalm 1:2-3, Galatians 5:22-23
6: **Spiritual Growth** ....Philippians 1:6, 1 Peter 2:2
7: **Messages to God** ....Deuteronomy 26:15
8: **A Room in Heaven** ....John 14:2-4
9: **Wide and Narrow Roads** ....Matthew 7:13-14, Luke 10:30-35
10: **Lost Sheep Hide-and-Seek** ....Luke 15:4-7
11: **Dancing David and Merry Miriam** ....Psalm 149:3-4, Psalm 150:4, Ecclesiastes 3:4, Lamentations 5:15, 2 Samuel 6:14-15, Exodus 15:20, Psalm 30:11
12: **Messenger Angels** ....Luke 2:10, Luke 1:13, Hebrews 13:2, Genesis 16:10, Genesis 22:11-12, Exodus 23:20, Judges 6, Acts 10:4-6
13: **Little Things Become God Things** ....Matthew 17:24-27
14: **Light in the Darkness** ....Matthew 5:14-16, John 1:4-5, Acts 26:17-18, Galatians 5:22-23
15: **A Strong Tower** ....Proverbs 18:10
16: **Honor Volleyball** ....1 Peter 2:17, Romans 12:10
17: **Let Jesus Help** ....Luke 5:4-11, John 21:3-8, Philippians 4:13
18: **The Early Church** ....Acts 8:1-3
19: **Birthday Cake for Jesus** ....Luke 2:11
20: **Traveling Nativity** ....Luke 2, Matthew 2
21: **Easter: Story Eggs** ....Luke 19-24
22: **Halloween: Pumpkin Parable** ....Romans 3:23, Revelation 3:20, John 1:29, Philippians 2:12-13, Matthew 5:16, 2 Corinthians 4:6, John 5:35
23: **Prayer Wall** ....Ephesians 6:18, Ephesians 2:20
24: **Overflow of the Heart** ....Matthew 6:22-23, Matthew 12:34-35
25: **The Throne** ....Revelation 12:7-9, Genesis 3:1-5, Exodus 32:1-10, Psalm 11:4, Revelation 3:21

Bubbles, Balloons, & Chocolate (PRESCHOOLERS)

1: **Lazarus** ....John 11:1-44
2: **Friends** ....Exodus 17:8-13
3: **Fishers of Men** ....Matthew 4:18-22, Acts 3:11-26, Matthew 28:16-20
4: **Invisible and Powerful** ....John 6:46, Romans 1:20
5: **Ezekiel** ....Ezekiel 2 and 3, Ezekiel 3:1-3
6: **Cross and Tomb** ....Matthew 27-28, Luke 24
7: **Dorcas Helping Others** ....1 Corinthians 13:4, Acts 9:36-42
8: **David and Goliath** ....1 Samuel 17
9: **Ark of the Covenant** ....Exodus 25:10-22, Deuteronomy 10:1-5, Joshua 3:14-17, 1 Samuel 6:1-16, 1 Kings 8:1-13, Revelation 11:19
10: **Angels are Powerful** ....Joshua 5:14, Luke 2:9-10, Luke 1:29-30, Luke 1:11-13
11: **Daniel in the Lions' Den** ....Daniel 6
12: **Cain** ....Genesis 4:1-15, James 4:7-8a
13: **Builders** ....Genesis 11:3-4, Nehemiah 2:12, Nehemiah 2:20, Nehemiah 4:6, Nehemiah 6:15-16
14: **Bubbles and Balloons** ....Ecclesiastes 2:10-11, Ecclesiastes 1:14, Matthew 6:19-21, Matthew 19:21, Matthew 5:44, Matthew 5:3-10, Matthew 10:30
15: **Sin—Missing the Target** ....Romans 3:23-24
16: **Samson** ....Judges 13-16
17: **Lot and Abraham** ....Genesis 11:27 to Genesis 19, Genesis 13:10-13, Genesis 13:18
18: **The Oatmeal Plague** ....Numbers 14:1-38, Numbers 13 and 14, Philippians 2:14
19: **Shine the Light of Jesus** ....John 1:9, Matthew 5:16
20: **Good and Bad Words** ....Proverbs 12:18, Proverbs 25:18, Proverbs 15:4, 1 Thessalonians 5:11
21: **The Expanding Egg** ....Acts 7:58, 8:1-3, 9:1-22
22: **Easter Calendar** ....Luke 19:28 to 24:12
23: **A Shepherd Knows His Sheep** ....John 10:3-14
24: **The Manger** ....Luke 2:7, Matthew 1-2, Luke 2
25: **Excess Baggage** ....Hebrews 12:1-2, Colossians 3:8, 1 Peter 2:1

Tried and True (TEENS)

1: **Be The One** ....Luke 17:12-19
2: **Walking Billboards** ....Romans 12:2, Philippians 4:8
3: **Christ The Ruler** ....John 14:6, John 8:31-32, John 7:16-17, John 3:5
4: **Bible Names and Places** ....Jeremiah 1:1-3
5: **Adversity** ....Genesis 37 and 39-45, Genesis 50:20, Psalm 34:18-19, 1 Peter 5:10
6: **Fear Factor** ....Joshua 1:9, Colossians 3:15
7: **Exciting Christians** ....2 Samuel 6:14-15, Matthew 14:13-14, 19
8: **Peter Walks on Water** ....Matthew 14:22-33
9: **Great Commission** ....Acts 1:8
10: **The Fire of the Holy Spirit** ....Acts 2:1-4, Philippians 2:12-13, Romans 7:14-15, John 14:26, James 5:14
11: **Write a Psalm** ....The Book of Psalms
12: **Easter: Passover Celebration** ....Exodus 12:3-13, Matthew 26:17-20
13: **Christmas Quiz** ....Luke 1-2, Matthew 1-2
14: **Last Words** ....Deuteronomy 32:46-47, Luke 24:50-51, Matthew 28:18-20
15: **Gender Differences** ....Genesis 1:27, Galatians 3:28, 1 Peter 3:7, Proverbs 5:7-14
16: **Lying is Dangerous** ....Acts 5:1-11, Proverbs 6:16-19
17: **Will It Float?** ....1 Timothy 4:12
18: **Proverbs** ....Proverbs 26:4-5, Proverbs 1:28, Proverbs 8:17
19: **Different Views** ....Matthew 26, Mark 14, Luke 22-24, John 12-20